Ancient Faith, Future Mission

ANCIENT FAITH, FUTURE MISSION

Fresh Expressions in the Sacramental Traditions

Edited by
Steven Croft, Ian Mobsby,
and Stephanie Spellers

Foreword by
The Most Reverend
Katharine Jefferts Schori

Seabury Books
NEW YORK

Cover design by Laurie Klein Westhafer
Typeset by K1 Creative

Library of Congress Cataloging-in-Publication Data

Ancient faith, future mission : fresh expressions in the sacramental
traditions / edited by Steven Croft, Ian Mobsby, and Stephanie
Spellers.
    p. cm.
Originally published: London : Canterbury Press, 2009.
Includes bibliographical references.

ISBN 978-1-59627-124-1 (pbk.)

1. Mission of the church. 2. Sacraments--Anglican Communion. I.
Croft, Steven J. L. II. Mobsby, Ian. III. Spellers, Stephanie.
BV601.8.A49 2010
234'.16--dc22

                    2009041976

First published in the United Kingdom in 2009 by The Canterbury
Press Norwich, Editorial office, 13–17 Long Lane, London, EC1A
9PN, UK. Canterbury Press is an imprint of Hymns Ancient and
Modern Ltd (a registered charity), St Mary's Works, St Mary's
Plain, Norwich, NR3 3BH, UK.

www.scm-canterburypress.co.uk

Published in the United States in 2010 by
Seabury Books
445 Fifth Avenue
New York, New York 10016

www.seaburybooks.com

An imprint of Church Publishing Incorporated
5 4 3 2 1

Contents

On the Ground

The Contributors

Foreword

KATHARINE JEFFERTS SCHORI

Fresh Expressions originated in the Church of England as a term for new and creative forms of Christian community. The term more often heard in North America is *emergent* or *emerging church*. In each context, the aim is to incarnate Christian worship and community in ways that the faith can be conveyed, understood and appropriated.

This movement certainly has roots in the liturgical reforms of the twentieth century, which sought to recover the original meaning, forms and dynamism of the early church's worship. More recent work and experimentation has sought to recover many strands from the church's broad tradition—icons, labyrinths, body prayer, monastic community, for example—amid the catholic recognition that no one strand is able to carry the whole of the tradition.

New worship forms are particularly consonant with the Anglican tradition, which has insisted since the Reformation that worship must be in a 'language understanded of the people.' Those reformation principles in turn have their origin in the abundantly contextualized Celtic Christianity which was remarkably effective at incarnating the faith in local forms. These emerging communities also seek to make the everyday the locus of faith, and often move toward a more communal form of Christianity, echoing the Celtic church and the desert and early monastic traditions.

All of which is to say that Fresh Expressions and emergent church are the latest iteration in an ancient and essential tradition, ways of telling the old, old story for the people of today.

Others have made the observation that the cultural expressions current in North America and Western Europe today are much more like the context of early Christianity than at any time since the early centuries of the Common Era. Scholars often call these current contexts post-Christian, having left the worlds of Christendom behind. The emergent Christian environment is also often post-colonial, beginning to recognize that local expression has its own intrinsic value, and a hegemonically imposed uniformity is not something to be sought after.

A further challenge emerges from post-Christian contexts, which provide little cultural reinforcement of Christianity. The generations born since the Second World War have increasingly been reared without any real knowledge of the great figures and foundational narratives of the Bible. Communicators of the faith today can no longer rely on general cultural knowledge of Christianity, and must instead introduce the faith in ways that do not expect any familiarity. Indeed, such familiarity with Christianity as may exist is often roundly dismissive, negative and even scornful, having been formed on the worst caricatures of TV preaching. Those communicators must earn an opportunity to be heard despite that negativity.

This slim volume is an introduction to the challenging and exciting work of evangelism in such contexts. It is about original or primary evangelism, rather than secondary. The vitality that the communities emerging from these contexts display is the result of that newly kindled fire (dare we say Pentecostal fire?). Like all of life, that vitality takes many different forms, each growing out of, or evolving from, the particular gifts and challenges of the local environment.

Solomon's Porch in Minneapolis is one such, a community almost hoary, now housed (or more accurately, couched) in its own building, and working to navigate the transition from original community to stable institution without losing that initial and essential fire. Another can be seen at St. Peter's in Carson City, Nevada, where the local creativity of music, liturgy and teaching has produced a multi-generational community that has something to do with what Archbishop of Canterbury

Rowan Williams has called a 'mixed economy church,' in this case a fresh expression in an old and staid worship space that is the epitome of conservative New England transplanted to the Wild West. Yet another, Transmission, has been emerging over several seasons in New York City, seeking to serve the local context, including the sex workers first served by a predecessor community, Holy Communion Episcopal Church, in the 1800s. It is now experimenting with cell group forms, new monasticism, and providing Easter worship for the larger community as a way of teaching and evangelizing.

Above all, this work is a matter of discerning the gifts of a local context, blessing the best of those gifts and responding to the hungers, and challenging the gathering community to learn from the many roots and strands of our faith. These gathered parts of the Body know deeply that God's image is present in all of creation, and do not hesitate to keep searching for it in unexpected places and people. Authentic Christian communities developing in this incubator demonstrate a hospitality that invites others in, seeking to discern their own gifts and in the process luring tourists to become fellow travelers on The Way of Jesus.

Always there is music, innovation, prayer, laughter, doubt, questions, discussion and discovery and, necessarily in those communities that endure, missional service to those beyond themselves. Christ is made real within the community gathered, who become God in the flesh, transforming the world.

Read, learn, question, seek wisdom and dream through these pages—and then go and do likewise, working to transform a hungry and searching world. A blessed and joyous journey!

KATHARINE JEFFERTS SCHORI
SEPTEMBER 2009

From the Editors

STEPHEN CROFT, IAN MOBSBY
AND STEPHANIE SPELLERS

The launch of the 'Mission-shaped Church' report by the Church of England in 2004 was a pivotal moment. It brought new focus to the Church's support of alternative, or 'fresh expressions', of church and an awareness of the need for a 'mixed economy', with the experimental working alongside the traditional. It is not often that consensus is reached quickly in the Church of England, but, on this occasion, it was. The Fresh Expressions team, led by the Archbishop's Missioner, was the immediate result. This was quickly followed by the development of local fresh expressions up and down the country, changes in law concerning what a legitimate form of church is, new Bishops' Mission Orders and the recognition of new forms of ministry with Ordained and lay Pioneer Ministry training. In response to the seismic changes in contemporary culture, and the new mission needs created, the face of the Church of England has undergone significant and rapid change.

The focus on fresh expressions has led to an increased ecumenicalism, with the Methodist Church joining as an equal partner in Fresh Expressions, the agency. More recently a number of other denominations have also entered negotiations to join with us, and, in fact, fresh expressions can now be found in many countries throughout the world, including Australia, Canada and the USA. In short, greater unity is emerging through the collaborative forms of mission and ministry fresh expressions encourage.

However, the 'Mission-shaped Church' report was never

a final word; it was more of an opening act to an unfolding calling. Developing local fresh expressions of church is a complicated business that requires ongoing theological reflection and exploration. An authentic mark of the church is its sacramentality. For mature forms of church to develop out of mission initiatives, pioneers need support, dialogue and critical reflection. Such exploration enables authentic expressions of church to grow by drawing on the richness of their tradition of origin, whilst reframing it within new cultural contexts. All church workers face the challenge of how to be authentic and yet become contextual, relevant and accessible. Developing a mature, contextual sacramentality and spirituality is therefore the pursuit of drawing on ancient faith traditions to meet contemporary, and future, mission needs.

This book seeks to explore some of the current issues and questions in the field, by drawing on the expertise of a number of pioneers, theologians and thinkers from various constituencies in the UK and USA. Most have a sacramental focus, and draw on catholic and/or contemplative perspectives. Both perspectives are vital for the rounded dialogue and exploration necessary to develop mature and authentic expressions of church. The book also contains the address of the Archbishop of Canterbury, and the reflections of Abbot Stuart Burns OSB, following the Fresh Expressions National Pilgrimage to Coventry Cathedral in December 2008, which sought to promote fresh expressions of the catholic and contemplative traditions.

All of the contributors have written from a personal perspective without being aware of each other's contributions. Although there is much agreement between the different contributions there are also some inevitable differences of emphasis. The views expressed should therefore be seen as those of the particular authors and not a common mind of all the authors together, or the editors, or the views of Fresh Expressions.

We would like to pay tribute to all those seeking to pioneer or to encourage fresh expressions of church in a catholic and contemplative tradition, and for the generous sharing of insights and wisdom represented by these essays. We are also grateful to Aaron Kennedy for his careful and efficient work as editorial assistant, and to Christine Smith and Canterbury Press for their support as publishers.

Our hope is that this book will encourage many would-be and well-established pioneers, enabling us all to dig deeper into the richness of our heritage, as we strive to meet the challenges of our times.

STEPHEN CROFT AND IAN MOBSBY

The movement to birth mission-shaped, sacramental Christian communities has taken different paths in the United States and the United Kingdom. The Church of England launched Fresh Expressions and later invited other denominations to come aboard as partners. Meanwhile, efforts in the USA emerged with far less institutional backing, often falling under the broad, trans-denominational umbrella of the emerging or emergent church or The Great Emergence.

The labels vary, and an ocean divides the two movements. In spirit they have always been intimately connected, with pioneers and thinkers collaborating like two streams running parallel, sometimes jumping the banks and flowing on the other side, only to return with fresh ideas and bigger questions. In this volume—first published in England, now updated for the American context—the rest of us are welcome to listen to this ongoing transatlantic conversation.

Like any cross-cultural exchange, some translation is necessary. For Americans, in particular, certain terms our British counterparts use will sound familiar but in fact signify a quite different meaning. In other cases, certain concepts that are now common for readers in England could use some unpacking for Americans. With that in mind, here is a brief glossary to clarify terms:

- **Mission-shaped Church:** As Mobsby and Croft explained earlier, 'Mission-shaped Church' is the title of a 2004 report by the Church of England's Mission and Public Affairs

Council. The term more generally refers to the formation of Christian communities that are literally shaped for mission, that is, geared to meet the specific cultural context in which we as contemporary, local missionaries are living out God's purposes. The goal is not mimicry of the culture, nor is it merely performing 'cool' liturgies or adding new bodies to old pews. Rather, the focus is on coherently proclaiming *and* practicing the reign of God. It is creating Christian communities that can effectively engage our wider communities in God's movement. It is walking alongside those neighbors who are already fulfilling God's dream in ways the Church never imagined. . . but could.

• **Fresh Expression:** A fresh expression is the embodiment of the mission-shaped church vision. It might not be a new congregation or a newly planted church. In fact, the 'Mission-shaped Church' report identifies several forms, such as alternative worship communities, café churches, cell churches, churches birthed out of community initiatives (including the restructuring or refounding of an existing church to serve a specific community), multiple and midweek congregations, traditional church plants, traditional forms of church inspiring new interest (including new monastic communities) and youth congregations. The goal is to have a mixed economy of forms, with traditional parishes and fresh expressions in close proximity and active conversation. One might think of it as biodiversity on an ecclesial scale. Archbishop Rowan Williams blessed just such a movement when he wrote in his Foreword to the 'Mission-shaped Church' report: If 'church' is what happens when people encounter the Risen Jesus and commit themselves to sustaining and deepening that encounter in their encounter with each other, there is plenty of theological room for diversity of rhythm and style, so long as we have ways of identifying the same living Christ at the heart of every expression of Christian life in common. (p. vii)

- **Catholic:** In America, Catholic usually means either Roman Catholic (capital C) or universal (lowercase c). Most Episcopalians understand themselves to be catholic, that is comprehensive, sacramental, liturgical, corporate, historic, contemplative and incarnational. However, given the Roman Catholic Church's dominance in our context, we tend to prefer one of those individual adjectives over 'catholic. In the UK, where the Church of England was founded as the English expression of the ancient Catholic Church—and Rome is seen as but one of several centers of catholic Christianity—the relationship to the word 'catholic' is less conflicted. Writers in this volume use the word quite freely and frequently. An American reader confused by the use of 'catholic' might insert the word 'liturgical,' which summons ancient tradition, sacramentality, embodiment and more. Then again, just as many leaders have expanded the idea of being 'evangelical,' perhaps American pioneers would benefit from more boldly claiming and fleshing out our 'catholic' identity.

In the end, there is no American way or English way. There certainly are no recipes or rulebooks. You are welcomed here to enter a conversation: first, with the leaders and pioneers who have contributed their stories and reflections; then, with the people and cultures that make up your own context; and just as importantly, with the traditions and dreams that have given our faith shape and texture for centuries. All these voices matter. Come close and listen.

STEPHANIE SPELLERS

References

Church of England Report, 2004, *Mission-shaped Church: Church Planting and Fresh Expressions of Church in a Changing Context*, London: Church House Publishing

Address to the Fresh Expressions National Pilgrimage, Coventry Cathedral

December 2008

ARCHBISHOP OF CANTERBURY, ROWAN WILLIAMS

Most people undoubtedly think of 'Fresh Expressions' as essentially something evangelical. They're right, of course, in one sense: this is about the good news, the 'evangel', and about how it becomes most clearly audible or visible. It would be quite something if the word 'evangelical' meant just that. The trouble is that it's become for so many people simply the badge of one kind of Christian. But, having said that, we should remember that exactly the same is true of 'catholic': what if *that* word brought to mind, not one kind of Christian among others, but that dimension of Christian life which is concerned with speaking the whole truth to the whole person – which is pretty much how St Cyril of Jerusalem defined the word in the fourth century?

'Catholic' and 'evangelical' are words that belong together when they're properly used, because the good news isn't particularly good if it isn't the whole truth for the whole person. But we have to recognize that the words have drifted apart and that they've so often been used in restrictive ways. 'Evangelical' has come to suggest both a narrow focus on the Bible and an anxious moralism; 'catholic' brings to mind a fussy and churchy style of Christianity, more interested in how worship looks than how it converts or transforms. And although all sorts of things in the last thirty or so years have changed these perceptions – not least the great changes in the Roman Catholic Church, the recovery of Scripture and the re-imagining of worship – the distortions persist.

Still, granted that there are historical differences between the range of ideas evoked by these two words, and granted that mission and evangelism are things that tend to get lumped with evangelical identity, what is there about the catholic identity that's positive, and, still more important, what are the positive things that are specially relevant to fresh expressions of church? In this piece I'll concentrate on four areas. Among the features people associate with catholic spirituality and theology are these:

- Catholics are concerned about non-verbal as well as verbal expressions of faith;
- they give a central place to sacramental action as a necessary way of proclaiming the Word;
- they have a strong sense of the need to see Christian life as something that takes time, that evolves over a period and is symbolized by the recurring journey of the Christian year; and
- they insist that faith is a community experience not only an individual one.

It's quite important to recognize that all of this is in fact deeply biblical – not just a cultural import into the 'simple' world of proclamation. The Bible is full of stories about God communicating through act and sign as well as language – or rather through the language *of* act and sign. One of the saddest and silliest legacies of some kinds of Reformation controversy is the idea that there is some sort of great gulf between God speaking in words and God speaking through events and things. The Bible shows God speaking through history itself before anything else; it shows God being incarnate in a speechless child before the message of the gospel is announced in words. Certainly we *need* the words to name and communicate what it is that is present in the speechless child; but once this has happened we can see that God's work is not only in words. When we say that the Word became flesh, we implicitly admit that it is the entire flesh and blood of Jesus that 'speaks' God – not just the moments when Jesus opens his mouth to say something. And this in turn helps us make sense of the way in which we are called as Christians to follow the whole path of Jesus' life; as Paul says in Philippians 2, having the 'mind' of Jesus is following his self-emptying journey 'from heaven to earth, from the earth to the cross, from the grave to the skies', as the song puts it. And in all this we are responding to Jesus' call not just to acquire a new set of ideas but to rejoin the people of God and to help reveal God to the world in the character of our life together. This is the basic material of Gospel and epistle alike, not to mention the Old Testament. It is very eccentric to reduce all this to a Christian 'message' simply announced in words, received by the mind and expressed in individual behaviour only.

Each of these features has a particularly marked significance in the context in which we are seeking to discover the possibility of fresh expressions of church. It's one of the clichés of our time that we live in an age that is not very receptive to 'book culture'. I actually think this is a bit of an overstatement; but the truth it contains is that, so far from being bound to communication through clear information economically expressed in words, our society is still deeply sensitive to symbols and inclined to express important feelings and perceptions in this way. Anyone who's ever looked at the little pile of flowers and other tributes that accumulates at the site of a traffic accident will realize that something is being said that doesn't lend itself to words, and yet is felt by people to be a necessary way of putting outside themselves the things that can't or mustn't stay inside – a way of communicating something. Of course there are dangers, because at some point we need at least to try and put into words what this is about, however inadequately, so as to be able to communicate it more fully and more truthfully; but this can't be hurried too much.

Similarly, the idea that Christian life is first a matter of acts rather than ideas alone rings bells with many aspects of where we are culturally. We show what we really mean by what happens in and through our bodies; we show our commitments most clearly when we put our bodies on the line, as we say. We may talk about solidarity with the poor, or our deep awareness of the ecological crisis; but where are we to be found? If we're found only in comfortable neighbourhoods or travelling in gas-guzzling machines, there is a bit of a mismatch (and yes, before anyone else points it out, I know I live in a palace and do lots of international air travel, and have to do a fair bit of work to retain any credibility in speaking about these matters). Once more, it is of the first importance that God makes himself credible to us by *where he is*, that is, in a body of vulnerable flesh, alongside the outcast, on the cross. He acts to tell us who he is; that's why he is trustworthy. God's dealings with us are events – and not just the sort of event where someone gives a lecture. And when the Bible uses the Greek word *ekklesia* for what happens when God speaks, this is the point it's making: the word means literally a calling-together. When God acts, the event that follows is like the rush of iron filings towards a magnet. Things are disturbed and the pattern of relationships changes. *This* is the Church. If we're thinking about the funny things that happen to words, think about the word 'ecclesiastical': it means for most of us (if we ever use it at all, that is) just churchy. Yet the original word behind it in the Bible is about this rush of filings to the magnet, a turbulence in the very air, like the day of Pentecost.

But of course when things rush together, in the real world of human experience, they take time to settle into a pattern. And this is perhaps where the catholic vision is most in tension with a lot of our contemporary world. So far, I've suggested that the raw materials of catholic identity are very much in tune with aspects of our world; but the one thing we are truly awful at is taking time, or understanding that some outcomes, some processes, just take the time they take – that you can't rush the business of growing. A lot of the misery in our economic crisis is the result of people more and more losing touch with time – the time taken to build trust, the time taken to bring a new enterprise to maturity and so the time taken to see an investment of energy and money bear fruit.

And many individuals would find it quite hard to know what you were talking about if you started trying to discuss how they made sense of their lives as a developing story, something unfolding over time. The temptation is to think you can always reinvent yourself and that you are what you say you are or what you'd like to be at any moment. It often takes a shock or a tragedy to remind you that your life really is made up of the accumulated effects of choices you may have forgotten, experiences you never registered or understood. Or perhaps in a crisis you realize that where you've been and who you've known has given you resources you didn't know you possessed. Most of the time, though, we live in the moment in a pretty unhelpful way, and it takes a difficult situation to make us see the dangers of living without roots.

Here the catholic insight is counter-cultural. We have, it says, a story, a drama to show you, and if you live inside it, letting your own life be lit up and shown to you afresh by it, you may find that it begins to mould your story and give you a new sense of what's possible. Here's the story of how the maker of everything became part of the world he'd made – letting go of his mystery and otherness to be one of us, so that we might find our way into the mystery and otherness of his love and discover a new way of being at home with ourselves and at home in the universe. This is a lifetime's work (at least), so it helps to have the basic story retold regularly. We find ourselves going around the same territory again and again, but always bringing different material and new memories to it, asking how this fresh experience or insight is going to settle down into the world mapped out by the central story.

Every year, the process is re-enacted. We begin by imagining ourselves in the world before Christ, longing for a release, a new horizon, a world of liberation whose nature we don't yet know. We celebrate the miracle of God arriving in flesh and blood in our world, and we trace his path through struggle and suffering to death, trying to shift our perspectives and change our priorities (trying to discover *metanoia* in biblical language) so that we see all this as the way into life and out of falsehood. We receive the shattering news that death cannot contain the flesh and blood of Jesus and cannot end the life-giving relationships he creates. And we find out that in the community where these relationships are recognized and thought about and lived out, we learn how to relate to God the Father as Jesus does and to understand that each of us is necessary to the life of the other – the communion of the Holy Spirit. Into this annual course of discovery we put our particular concerns and changes and new perspectives, and it dawns on us slowly that we are finding out who we are by finding out who Jesus is – and vice versa.

Taking time to grow through all this is absolutely bound up with the business of learning from each other, and so recognizing that we need each other. And this is both counter-cultural and deeply resonant in our world. We in the modern 'West' live in what is in all kinds of ways a very individualistic environment, where the freedom to become exactly what you want to be, when you want, is often presented as the best thing there is. Yet the sense of isolation, of no one really wanting to take responsibility for others, produces a frightening feeling of things being fragmented, and people can get very nostalgic about 'community'. The catholic tradition in Christianity looks as though it invests pretty heavily in community, and in many ways it does; but it also says that community isn't just a warm huddle that reassures us. It's a place in which we have to learn to be honest (hence all those catholic disciplines of spiritual formation – self-examination, confession and so on), and it's a community that is always pushing us beyond our comfort zones, because it's a community existing by God's invitation and God's faithful accompaniment, not our own sense of what will make us feel safe. We're always struggling to keep up with God's movement outwards to reach all human beings; he's always ahead of us, already talking to the people we hoped we wouldn't have to meet.

Now all this suggests that catholic identity has a huge amount to say to the fresh expressions world – and, perhaps a bit surprisingly, that it helps get a rather different picture of what 'church' means. Or, put it another way, it prompts the question, 'What does it take to make a church, for a church to be *there*?' A good catholic theology of the Church starts well back beyond any issues around institutions; it starts by asking how a community embodies, practically and visibly, some of the things we've been thinking about. It starts by acknowledging that 'church' is an event – a calling together; and that when this calling together has happened, what follows is a set of acts and words that get us walking in step with Jesus, praying his prayers, living his life, not as a matter of historical reconstruction but as a kind of singing in tune with his eternal relation with his Father. Church is where the Son's journey from the Father's heart into death and hell, and back again, is lived out.

And the sacraments of the Church are there not as mysterious rituals to deepen our sense of group identity – though of course they do that among other things. They are there to tell us what story it is that defines the shape of our world, and to take us further on our journey, on our following out the Son's journey. Something is needed to anchor what we're doing in what God is doing – in the event that is God's action, not ours. And the sacraments of Baptism and Holy Communion simply announce that *here* something is being done that isn't our work. We pour the water; God accepts us as sons and daughters. We pray over the bread and wine and share them; God renews in us the gift of his Son's life and hears our prayers as if they were Christ's, taking us for a moment into the fully reconciled joy that awaits us at the end of all things. Church is not primarily an event in which we do something, think something, feel something; it is being together in a situation where we trust God to do something and to change us – whether or not we notice it, let alone fully understand it.

That's why, whatever the practical problems, one of the questions that fresh expressions of church have to deal with is how to manage this crossover from what we do to what God does;

how to create an environment in which church can happen in the fullest sense, with the sacramental life flowing through as a sign and channel of God's action. Because the Catholic ought to be able, believe it or not, on the basis of what we've been thinking about, to sit very light to quite a lot of the externals of institution and form, the Catholic is in a good position to break the mould and concentrate on what sort of environment allows God the space to be God, actively and transformingly. The universal, recognisable signs, the presence of recognisable people (ordained ministers) whose responsibility it is to keep these signs in focus and see that they happen – this is not a matter of mechanical requirements imposed on a spontaneous human gathering, but of how the human gathering remembers that it isn't ever *just* a human gathering. Properly understood, the sacramental life in a congregation is inseparable from the impulse to silence, adoration, willingness to receive – all the things that break us free from the tyranny of hectic activism and trying to achieve. It goes with all those things we discussed earlier about how catholic practice both resonates with and fundamentally challenges so much of our current cultural scene.

And that, finally, is a central aspect of what is good news, what is evangelical, about a catholic approach to fresh expressions of church. Evangelicals are rightly passionate about the supremacy of grace and the fact that we are not saved by human effort; Catholics affirm that for this to go on being real for us, we need, not just better communication strategies, more lively language or more up-to-the-minute activities, important as these are, but practices – such as Baptism and Eucharist, where Scripture truly becomes contemporary happening – that anchor us in the fleshliness of the Word who became human, in the story of the time he took and takes to bring us home to his Father, in the awareness of our need for each other. The practical challenges are legion, as we all know; but a genuine catholic vision of the Church can give us indispensable resources for seeing the Church in its fullness, flexibly and hopefully, because it makes us see it in, and only in, the light of God's own action.

8

2

One, Holy, Catholic and Fresh?

BRIAN MCLAREN

The Christian community in the UK is, I believe, of pivotal importance to Christian mission in the world. When British Christians are wise, courageous, faithful and creative, the rest of us will benefit. British Christians are uniquely positioned to lead the way among Western nations in engaging with the massive shift in global culture that is currently associated with the prefix *post*: postmodern, post-colonial, post-Christendom, post-Communist, post-national, post-Enlightenment, and so on.

Some might be surprised for me to say this, especially as a US citizen. Perhaps they would say that the 'ring of power' passed from the UK to the US after World War II, so that the headquarters of empire on planet earth are found in the US, on Wall Street, in the Pentagon, and in Hollywood. They might make the additional case that America's religious influence, extended, for example, through religious broadcasting, has an imperial tone to it as well. Where that is true, I would say it is generally for the worse, because America is an anomaly in many ways. The Christian community in the US has in many ways managed to maintain itself in a kind of echo chamber or change-resistant bubble of Christendom – a bubble that will eventually burst, one way or another. Both fundamentalist and institutional Protestantism in the US maintain at the core a pre-1960 view of the world and of the Church's engagement with it, and this isn't the way forward.

England, on the other hand, has already seen its bubble burst. For that reason, it is a nation that has gone through the more normative pattern of change we may call the postmodern/post-colonial transition, or perhaps the post-Christendom transition.

That's why for people who want to prepare the Church for the future – whether they're in Birmingham, UK, or Birmingham, Alabama; whether they're in England or New England; whether they're in London and Perth in the UK, or East London (RSA) or Perth (Australia) in the southern hemisphere – I believe England provides a tremendous laboratory to test new ideas and learn from them. What is said (or sung) of New York is true of England: if an idea or approach can make it there, it can make it anywhere (almost) in the world beyond modernity and Christendom.

(Of course, we need to remember that a large part of the world functions in a non-modern or pre-modern mindset, and a large part of the world is just entering and getting comfortable with a modern mindset. But barring a reversion into world war or some other catastrophe, the momentum through modernity into something post-al seems likely to continue.)

It's been said that the road to the future goes through the past – that we cannot move forward without reaching back – and that is especially true in this time of change. Many of the resources we need for the postmodern world lie in the pre-modern world. Many of the resources we need for the post-Constantinian world lie in the pre-Constantinian world. So this postmodern moment is a good time for church leaders in the UK to recall the pre-modern vision of the Church embodied in the creedal language of 'one, holy, catholic, and apostolic church'.

The Christian community in the UK – drawing from its pre-modern Anglican and Celtic heritage – has invaluable resources in these four profound words. I'm hopeful that Christians around the world will learn and benefit from the Anglican embodiment of one, holy, catholic, and apostolic.

One Church: the global way

'One Church' in the New Testament meant an unprecedented coming together of Jews and Gentiles in the kingdom of God.

It meant that the most profound divisions in human society – between male and female (sexual divisions), Jew and Greek (religious and cultural divisions), slave and free (class divisions) – were transcended 'in Christ' – which means 'in the liberating king' – which means 'in the kingdom of God'.

Today, sexual, religious, cultural and class divisions still divide humanity: male/female, gay/straight, Christian/Muslim/Jew/Hindu, believer/atheist/agnostic, West/rest, rich/poor, have/have-not, and so on. With nuclear, biological, and chemical weapons in play, intensified by the realities of terrorism and counter-terrorism, these divisions have the potential to explode into a world-engulfing catastrophe. Now more than ever we need the Christian community to proclaim and embody a vision of unity that transcends these divisions. In Paul's words, we must believe that Jesus himself is our peace, and that he has made the two one, destroying the dividing wall of hostility, creating in himself one new humanity.

Seeking to manifest this unity in our day, we must acknowledge the reality that we live in a post-colonial moment – in the aftermath of centuries of colonialism. For the global south – the formerly colonized – this means assessing the damage done by centuries of being dominated and exploited. For the global north – the former colonizers – this means assessing the damage done by centuries of dominating and exploiting. Just as alcoholism scars both the family members and the alcoholics themselves, colonialism scars both parties in ways more and less obvious.

These scars can't be minimized. They must be fully acknowledged if they are truly to heal. And the UK has, to a degree that becomes apparent when contrasted with the parallel lack of awareness in the US, begun that process of assessing the downsides of colonialism, on its colonies and on itself. This assessment no doubt is far from complete, but it is nonetheless real, and brings with it a global sensitivity that many nations do not possess. For example, where I live, it's virtually impossible to get good global news: when we want to see what's happening beyond our shores, we turn to the BBC.

The great emergence in which we are all participants (or against which many are resisters) invites us to step up to a higher perspective, to emerge from individual self-interest, above tribal or ethnic or religious self-interest, and above national self-interest, to a concern for the global common good. Whether it's Bono reminding us that Africa's emergency is our emergency, CMS reminding us that the world's poor are our neighbours, Steve Chalke reminding us that our love for Christ is measured by our love for the least of these, or Tony Blair reminding us that the deadly dance of terrorism and counter-terrorism can plunge us into a nuclear war that reduces our planetary future ... we're at a point where we must realize that our biggest problems are not us-versus-them problems, but rather us-versus-us problems. In other words, we are all addicted to fossil fuels. We are all participants in a runaway military-industrial complex, and in related cycles of fear, resentment and violence. We are all tempted to forget the poor, but they will not be forgotten, one way or another.

Perhaps it's an advantage of living on a relatively small island, or a consequence of having so many large immigrant populations (making curry a national dish in England), or the aftermath of holding a global empire, but for whatever reason, British Christians seem less likely to forget the global networks – ecological, economic, political, social and spiritual – to which we all belong and through which we are all relatives.

To be one global Church is very different in a post-colonial setting. In a colonial mindset, the Church in the rest of the world learned to live by the normative standards set in the West. In a post-colonial setting, we seek true equality and collegiality among leaders from West and East, North and South. There is give-and-take, an awareness that one-size-fits-all solutions are seldom as viable as they were under colonialism. This isn't easy, as recent struggles in the Anglican Communion make clear. But we must make the shift from a Eurocentric Christianity to a truly global Christianity, and the recent struggles – as painful as they are – are actually signs not of failure but of success in facing the struggle of moving forward. They're growing pains, progress pains, labour pains as the Church as a truly global community is being born.

A Holy Church: the ancient contemplative way

Christian faith was severely reduced in the modern Western Church; it gradually shrank from a robust, integrated and generous way of life into a rigid, restrictive and exclusive system of belief. Our vision was constricted to one right answer for every question, one right interpretation for every text, one right opinion on every controversy. This constricting and ungenerous approach to orthodoxy created a feeding frenzy of division: *Our church is more doctrinally correct than your church! Your church is less doctrinally correct than ours! We're separating ourselves from you!*

This verse-parsing, fault-finding, stone-casting spirit did not lead to greater purity and beauty in the Church: it led to greater ugliness. Ugly division. Ugly arrogance. Ugly pettiness. Ugly schism.

No doubt, at the fringes, Anglicans have experienced this self-consuming division process along with other Protestants. But at the core, Anglicans have been repulsed by the ugliness of it all. At the core, they have sought to retain the grand and robust beauty of holiness. And in particular, they have cherished ancient liturgy as a way of doing so. By centring on worship – liturgical worship, with a contemplative leaning, with a taste for the beautiful – Anglicans were less infatuated with attempts to shrink-wrap the mysteries of God and gospel in tidy, little, square verbal packages; like the Psalmist, the one thing they desired, the one thing they sought above all others was the beautiful holiness of God. If the locus of constricting religion is in books, the locus of Anglican religion is in liturgy. If the one is focused on argument and correctness, the other is focused on reverence and awe.

In the pursuit of this kind of spirituality, the Celtic era of Anglican Christianity has been a special resource to Anglicans, consciously or subconsciously, directly or indirectly. Now I'm sure that some portion of interest in all things Celtic is simply a fad. But I'm also sure that beneath the fad there is substance.

The Celtic tradition was always a kind of resistance movement, countering encroachment from alien influences. In its origins, Celtic Christianity was defined by resisting Greco-Roman assimilation. It refused to surrender to Platonism, and instead saw the glory of God in the material world. It refused to surrender to Roman chauvinism, which upheld Roman warrior culture as 'civilized' and everything else as 'barbarian'. It maintained this resistance by celebrating the Spirit of God's pleasure in being incarnating into Celtic culture, not just Greco-Roman culture. It refused to let the faith be reduced to a kind of doctrinal combat zone. Having tasted in worship the mystery and beauty that always take us beyond words, it retained a mystical attitude that kept its leaders from taking their verbal faith-formulations too seriously.

Like the Celtic movement, the postmodern transition involves a resistance to a dominating elite. Just as the Celts resisted Roman hegemony, the emergent Christian community resists the ongoing encroachment and domination of Western modernity. By 'getting enlightened about the Enlightenment', the postmodern frame of mind deconstructs rather than defends modern categories and assumptions. It resists the constriction and reduction of faith into mere statements and doctrinal systems: it believes that God's truth can never be separated from beauty, nor can God's beauty be separated from truth, and in that fusion of truth and beauty, there is the mysterious glow of holiness.

This resistance to modern reductionism is, I believe, absolutely necessary, but it also poses dangers for Christians who have no memory of what precedes modernity. If everything you know of Christian faith is interwoven with threads of modernity, how can you untangle your faith from modernity without your whole faith unravelling? Having strong pre-modern threads helps a great deal. I believe this is a time to cherish as never before those pre-modern threads in our tapestry of faith

– such as the pre-modern and especially Celtic threads that the Anglican community retains.

Catholic Church: the middle way

In its aspiration to be one global community the Church will not find it easy to resist being divided by denominational and nationalist ties. In cherishing the beauty of holiness, the Church will need to work hard to resist having its soul reduced to a list of correct doctrines. To resist these constrictions and reductions, the Church must hold to another ancient value: catholicity.

There are two models of catholicity. One is a colonial or imperial model: unity and universality are maintained by submission to one dominating will. The other is the humble or charitable model: unity and universality are maintained by a generous spirit of inclusion. This spirit of inclusion is, at its core, a refusal to practice elitism.

It's interesting to look at the key divisions in church history in this light. The ancient Church was remarkably able to tolerate diversity. There was room for Tertullian to ask, 'What has Athens to do with Jerusalem?' and room for Justin to assert, 'Socrates was a Christian before Christ.' There was room for Tatian to describe Christian faith as a barbarian movement (as opposed to a Greco-Roman movement), and for Clement to describe Christian faith as the true philosophy to which Greco-Roman culture aspired but never attained. The Church could tolerate diversity, but it could not tolerate elitism. Diversity could enrich the unity of the Church, but elitism destroyed it.

So heretical movements became schismatic not simply by holding different opinions, but by claiming that they were the 'true' Christians, the 'pure' Christians, while all who didn't join them were inferior or sub-Christian. Their elitism was inherently intolerant, and the Church – to remain inclusive – could not tolerate elitist intolerance. Catholicity, in this sense, means a kind of populism; it means a church 'for the rest of us'.

The historic Anglican community, while it has had at its

fringes its fair share of extremists of various sorts, has by and large learned to choose the middle way. It learned this lesson the hard way in part, with blood being spilt in Christian-on-Christian violence on many occasions. But it also learned this lesson by watching the Thirty Years War decimate much of Europe: England managed to restrain itself from that full baptism in bloodshed by finding a both/and approach to the Reformation.

The English Church both welcomed and resisted the wild new ideas coming from Germany and Switzerland. It sought to accommodate (if not welcome) the new while preserving the old. More recently, more than any Christian community on the planet, I think, the Christian community in the UK at large welcomed the charismatic movement. And yet it did so without becoming full-blown Pentecostal: Anglicans, Methodists and Baptists stayed Anglican, Methodist and Baptist when they migrated to a more experiential posture to the Holy Spirit – another both/and, another middle way. Even now, there is a centre that holds English Christians together when they disagree on questions of human sexuality. Some see this as compromise, but I see it as wisdom.

While we Americans have a reactive habit of spinning off polarizing extremes (and exporting them globally), Christians in Britain seem to be able to find a centre that can hold. I'm sure much of this has to do with the stabilizing role of the Anglican Church in England, and in recent years, her wise and magnanimous Archbishop of Canterbury, not to mention the sagely role of John Stott. (I imagine it has to do with other traits of national character as well, perhaps including your ability to dissipate aggression through sport rather than religion!) It is a tremendously important instinct in times when any number of controversies could tempt us to turn on each other, rather than turn with each other, toward a world in great need.

This ability to resist elitism, to hold a centre, to follow a middle way, to avoid reactivity, to work 'above the line' as I describe it in one of my books (*New Kind of Christian*), is an exemplary trait that I hope the rest of us learn from.

Apostolic: the fresh way

The word apostolic, like the word catholic, can be taken in two ways. It can be taken in terms of apostolic succession, claiming elite legitimacy through purity of lineage and ordination. But it can also be taken in terms of apostolic mission – which is actually a kind of redundancy, since 'apostolic' and 'mission' both have to do with 'sent-in-ness'.

This idea of sent-in-ness is far more radical than most of us realize. The called-out-ness of the Church, taken alone, could be understood as a kind of favouritism: *we Christians are called out to be God's favourites*. But what if called-out-ness is actually a matter of being trained and equipped in preparation for being sent back into the world for service? Now, instead of being God's favourites, we are God's fellow-workers, God's allies in mission to the world.

The word people are using to capture this idea – that we are called-out-so-we-can-be-sent-back-in – is *missional*. Sadly, it's already become a kind of buzzword in many settings, meaning little more than 'really serious about evangelism' or 'intentional' or 'cool and hip'. If we are careful to really grasp the radical and profound theology that lies beneath the idea of missional, we realize it is another way of saying apostolic.

If the pure-lineage understanding of apostolic dominates, the Church will be inherently conservative. But if the sent-in-on-mission understanding prevails, the Church becomes inherently adaptive and flexible, shaping its forms and activities around mission rather than convention.

That's why I'm so thrilled about the Fresh Expressions movement in the UK. In light of the radical change into which our world is being swept – by advances in transportation, terrifying 'progress' in weaponry, unprecedented breakthroughs in communication, and the dynamic spiritual milieu of our post-Protestant and post-Catholic world – the Fresh Expressions movement is shaping the Church around this 'called-to-be-sent' and 'blessed-to-be-a-blessing' understanding of apostleship.

The apostolic/missional way follows the rather obvious (but

not widely recognized) truth that our greatest treasure is not our wineskins, but our wine. If we believe that the fresh wine of the gospel is ever-fresh, then we will realize that every wineskin is destined to serve for a while and then be discarded for the sake of the wine. When the old container grows rigid and inflexible, what are church leaders to do? They have three options, I believe.

1 Wait until it's too late. Wait until the wineskin ruptures and the wine is lost.
2 Throw out the old wineskin when it's too early. If we discard the old wineskin before we have a new one in place, ready to receive the wine of the gospel, the wine will likewise be lost.
3 Develop the new wineskin while the old wineskin is still working, so that the wine may be transferred before the old wineskins burst.

My guess is that most religious institutions follow option 1, and many would-be renewalists follow option 2. Relatively few, I think, choose the only viable option. Doing so requires leaders, in a real sense, to compete with themselves, to set up a new form that competes with the inherited form. But this self-competition is actually the only path to self-continuation. It also requires leaders to – in the cause of an absolute call to mission – relativize their forms as human constructions because they value the gospel wine as undeconstructible – as God-given and in that sense absolute.

When I was a pastor, I worked toward option 3 from a non-denominational context. That meant that we had great freedom to create new wineskins (within the subtle but strict limits imposed by the 'radio-orthodoxy' of American religious broadcasting, which is another story). It also meant that we had to find bridge elements from the tradition and borrow them. For us, that meant that we liberally incorporated the Book of Common Prayer into our worship services, especially the eucharistic liturgy. At that time, in the late 1980s and early 1990s, we were going against the flow, when 'seeker sensitivity' was all the rage, advocating that all vestiges of church culture be jettisoned (and exchanged for features of TV-Broadcast culture).

Frankly, I found relatively few non-denominational friends who shared my belief that we needed to incorporate the ancient with the avant-garde in pursuit of option 3. And I found even fewer examples of denominational leaders following option 3. Until, that is, I visited England to speak at the Greenbelt Festival several years ago.

I don't know how it happened (apart from providence), but I ended up with a few free hours, and bumped into Bishop Graham Cray, who also had a few free hours. We walked together among the array of tents and food vendors, and Graham explained to me the white paper on 'Mission-shaped Church' that would soon be published. I remember several times interrupting with questions that began like this: 'You can't be saying that you're going to ...' And he would reply, with a wry smile, 'That's exactly what we're saying.' There I learned about this amazing idea – an actual option 3 strategy – for an ancient institutional Church to experiment with fresh expressions of church alongside the inherited expressions; to create new wineskins while the existing wineskins were still in use; to compete with themselves (in a non-competitive way).

Some years later, I was in Norway. I had dinner with a half-dozen Lutheran pastors who had all started 'a new kind of church' within the state Church context. They were all enthusiastic and rejuvenated by their experience. I said, 'This reminds me of something I heard about in England from Bishop Graham Cray.' They laughed and said, 'Well, he came here and inspired us a few years ago.'

The one, holy, and catholic church must – if it is to be truly apostolic or missional – be ever-fresh. If it refuses freshness, it will, like a rigid, stiff wineskin, split. Its wine will spill out, leaving a hollow shell that is empty and lightweight. So, in many ways, the first three characteristics – one, holy, and catholic – can only be maintained if we are also missional and fresh. Put them together, and you have a four-part harmony and a full-colour picture through which the beauty of Jesus Christ can sing and shine.

3

New Monasticism

IAN ADAMS AND IAN MOBSBY

We wish to inspire a vision of another way of life. We want to stir up in some the idea of a mission, so that there will be lay missionaries to preach ... for the good life, other Moses', other St. Francis', and other St. Benedict's.
(Dorothy Day, 1946, pp. 1, 6, 8)

Dorothy Day and the Catholic Worker Movement are in a long tradition of activist Christian communities that have taken inspiration from the great pre-modern monastics. These predominantly lay communities have a strong commitment to a shared rhythm of life with a focus on justice and radical hospitality. Many practice radical forms of community whilst remaining actively part of the wider Church. All around the world, the twenty-first century has seen many new expressions of church emerge as part of what is being called 'new monasticism'. In common with traditional forms of monasticism, they share a desire to be incarnational – to follow Christ into the complexity of the world – and the belief that contemplative practices of prayer, hard work and worship have something to offer. Like the pre-modern friars, new-monastics – in their own technological and consumptive postmodern culture – have a passion to engage with people, particularly the poor. Further, they recognize that their globalized context has created a culture that is economically rich yet spiritually impoverished.

New research suggests that the cultural combination of consumerism and information technology has created a new spiritual hunger that stems mostly from a devotion to material possessions that cannot answer the existential questions of life (Mobsby, 2007, pp. 24–6, 38–9). Mental illness, addiction, loneliness and unhappiness are more prevalent than ever, and many are now searching for something of greater depth than a purely consumptive lifestyle (Mobsby, 2007, pp. 38–40; 2008, pp. 83–96). Therefore a new kind of techno-consumptive-mysticism is arising which, surprisingly, has much in common with the spirituality of pre-modernity (Mobsby, 2007, pp. 41–3, 46–7). It is into this increasingly superstitious culture of mysticism that both the traditional and postmodern friars are called to minister, enabling people to shift from being spiritual tourists to co-travelling Christian pilgrims through the practise of radical love, hospitality and action. Unsurprisingly then, new monastic communities tend to draw heavily on the spiritual resources of the contemplative and catholic traditions, reframing them in the context of our postmodern world.

What is new monasticism?

New monasticism is an outward facing, missional movement that, in common with early eremitical (hermit-alone) monasticism, emerged from the common source and ancient impulse to seek after and to serve God with wholehearted devotion. The outworking of this common inheritance of religious life broadly follows two distinct paths. The first is that of withdrawal, retreat and sanctuary. This is religious life as walled garden, as cloister, as monastery, and it is characterized by a long-term commitment to its setting. The shapers of this tradition are monks, nuns and all religious orders that prize stability. The other path is that of journey, presence and engagement. Religious life here is lived on the road in conversation with the stranger and through public action in the town square. The shapers of this tradition are friars and all the religious orders that seek to move outwards in mission.

New monastics have more in common with the friar tradition in that they seek to engage lovingly and creatively with the world as it is, in all its messy wonder. They continue to take much inspiration from each of the four ancient orders: from the Dominicans – the black friar preachers – they are learning hospitality and evangelism; from the Carmelites – the white friars – the importance of authentic spirituality; from the Augustinians they gain the impetus towards a 'rule of life'; and from the Franciscans the commitment to love, to practice social justice, and to cross boundaries in the name of Christ. Therefore, new monastics travel the physical, social and electronic networks of their world with the primary motivation of encounter and engagement with people, wherever they happen to be.

We might say that Benedict and Francis espoused fresh expressions of the Church of their day – they practised radical forms of community whilst remaining part of the wider Church. If the Church is pictured as a circle within the wider world, the Franciscans, says Fr Richard Rohr,[1] have always been on 'the edge of the inside' of that circle; this is a position also familiar to the new monastics. They belong to the Church but have deep connections to what lies beyond, in the world.

New monastic communities invariably remain part of the denomination to which they belong, and are committed to its accountability structures. However, because of their place 'out there' in culture – in common with their monastic forebears – they are also uniquely placed to offer new insights to the Church of which they are part. Their place 'on the edge of the inside' means that new monastic movements have a grounded place of belonging, a fertile opportunity to offer the gospel beyond the margins of church life, and a distinct role in helping the wider Church recover aspects of its life that have been forgotten, or not yet embraced. In new monastic communities we repeatedly find a sense of ancient memory being re-awakened. They recognize, as George Guiver says, that 'Our traditions are ancient and ingrained. They make us what we are to an extent that would astonish us if we could see it' (1990, p. 36). At a time when there is a widespread recognition that humanity (and the planet) has lost as much as it has gained through the achievements of modernity, the possibility of returning to a still centre through a renewed exploration of the monastic stream has deep appeal.

New monastic communities are very aware that they are just scratching the surface of the tradition, which is perhaps inevitable given that they are comprised of lay people who generally have day jobs and many other roles to fulfil. Nevertheless, there does appear to be an authentic commitment to living out the monastic tradition in imaginative and respectful ways. Contrary to some commentators, we will argue that new monasticism does not represent a dumbing down of the monastic tradition.

As a movement new monasticism is not cohesive or unified; it operates in a low-key way, and generally at a grassroots level. Gradually, however, its adherents are discovering, in the care of the ever-surprising Holy Spirit, that they are on similar, if not identical tracks. This is, of course, in the manner and spirit that many of the formal religious orders discovered their distinct charism and calling.

The Episcopal Church of the Apostles, a new monastic community in Seattle, states on its website:

> We value the traditions handed on to us that are of the gospel. We hold them as treasure entrusted to us for future generations. We will use them creatively to illumine the path we are walking within the emerging culture and towards the kingdom of God.
>
> ('About: Values', 2008)

'mayBe', a new monastic community in Oxford, states that it is: 'a community following in the way of Jesus by prayer, action and blessing for a better world now'. 'Safe Space', a community in Telford, wants 'to model [itself] as a monastic core, living by a rhythm and rule, spirit and scripture' ('Spirit of mayBe', 2008)

Members of 'Safe Space' in Telford desire 'to model ourselves as a monastic core living by a rhythm and rule, spirit and scripture' ('Core Principles', 2008).

This low-key movement should not be seen as a threat to church; rather, it should be embraced for its ability – in common with traditional monasticism – to bring new energy and life to the wider body, through the rediscovery of ancient, perhaps forgotten insights.

Authenticity in an age of self-construction

In our new, emerging context it has become a cultural norm to view identity as being individually and personally constructed. We live in times where the individual is valued over and above the community or wider society. People are searching for holistic wholeness, or rather the integration of work, home and relational areas of life. Being authentically whole has much to do with the current search for an authentic spirituality in which to define the self.

As is evident in the popularity of the Mind Body and Spirit Festivals, people are now exploring all sorts of spiritualities in the hope of finding something that works for them, something that brings inner peace and a sense of wholeness. In this context the authenticity of monasticism has renewed appeal, because its ancient practices and spirituality enable people to feel more centred. The challenge for new monastics is to open up the ancient contemplative traditions so that people can seek God in a wholehearted way, in love, simplicity and devotion. Some of the other spiritualities on offer today are seen as fake, or at least lacking depth, and many people now long for an authentic form of contemplative awareness.

Marie McCarthy defines this contemplative awareness as:

Grounded in discipline … [that] opens us to levels of reality not immediately apparent. It enables us to see ourselves, our circumstances, our world without illusion, to see without prematurely judging both the terrors of our present situation and the greatness of our possible inner evolution … It requires stillness, receptivity, and availability.
(McCarthy, 1999, pp. 199, 200)

This contemplative awareness is not about withdrawal; on the contrary, it requires action and participation in the world, and is essentially concerned with enabling people to shift from self-centredness to an awareness of God and the needs of others.

> Genuine contemplative awareness does not lead to a withdrawal from the world, but a deep immersion in the world ... Authentic spirituality, then, is marked by a dynamic relationship between contemplation and action which works toward the healing of the world and the wellbeing of all creation.
> (Pattison and Woodward, 1999, p. 200)

So what are the practices of contemplative, catholic spirituality, reframed for a postmodern context, that enable people to shift from spiritual tourism to pilgrimage?

Simplicity in a context of complexity

> You want to follow Christ, and not look back: remember that, as you walk in his footsteps you will be irresistibly drawn to share, and to a great simplicity of life.
> (Roger, 2000, p. 18)

We want to suggest that this grassroots movement is so attractive because it offers simplicity in a context of complexity. Our lives are multi-stranded, all of our actions solicit reactions, and almost all our decisions involve a compromise of some sort. New monastic communities articulate a desire to live more simply, to cause less damage to the individuals involved and to the wider world: they often keep a collective purse, they have minimal possessions, and they maintain a spiritual rhythm of life. Consequently, while owning less, they have a greater sense of abundance; happiness is found in the grand gesture, but also the small details of mundane, everyday life.

The Anglican priest and poet, R. S. Thomas, was writing

from a parish setting but his poem 'Gift' resonates with the
experience of many in the religious life:

Some ask the world
and are diminished
In the receiving
Of it. You gave me

Only this small pool
that the more I drink
from, the more overflows
me with sourceless light
(Thomas, 1995, p. 486)

New monastic communities embrace the 'small pool' of their
setting without any desire to create sprawling empires; they are
happy to have a low profile.

A sacramental understanding of life and time

The last few years have seen a growing awareness in culture
that all of life should be seen as holy and sacred. Of course
most would not describe it in those terms, preferring instead
words such as meaningful, energizing and holistic. Whatever
the terms used, the simplistic binary opposition of the sacred
and secular has been increasingly challenged. Spiritual tourists
now seek the sacred in the secular, normally through a consumptive lifestyle. This appears to be driving what Barry Taylor has called the sacralization of culture, where anything and
everything can have spiritual significance (2008, pp. 160-1)

New monastics – including emerging, and some fresh expressions of church – through their engagement with sacralized culture, draw increasingly on a sacramental worldview.

Emerging churches tend to have rediscovered a more sacramental approach to everyday life ... We gather around
weekly Eucharist ... We try to take a sacramental view of

the whole of creation ... A sacramental life is life lived in God, so each day is sacramental and we ourselves are sacraments of God in the world ... A defining characteristic of church has to be the regular participation in the community in Eucharist.
(Mobsby, 2007, p. 59)

The monastic way is centred on the belief that all of life is holy. Prayer and the Eucharist are of course at the heart of the monastic way of life, but work, rest, and re-creation are also important. Seeking to live in a way that honours all of life as holy changes us for the better; we become more whole, more fully human, even holy, through living each day with love and respect.

Many of the new monastic communities in the UK have formalized these practices and aspirations in the form of a rhythm of life. This is a reworking of traditional monastic vows of poverty, chastity and obedience. For example, the Moot Community in London has a rhythm with six elements: presence, acceptance, creativity, balance, accountability and hospitality (Mobsby, 2008, pp. 77–9). The hOME community in Oxford has reworked poverty as simplicity, chastity as purity, obedience as accountability and stability as presence. The great advantage of such a monastic rhythm is that it enables spiritual tourists to belong and therefore experience the sacramental way of life, worship and prayer, before having worked out if they believe. In this way people can seek and encounter God in the ordinariness of every day, and experience the presence of God and the Holy as part of an authentic sacramental spiritual community.

Teach us to pray

Prayer is the beginning, the middle and the end of all good; prayer illuminates the soul, and enables it to discern between good and evil.
(St Francis, XI)

27

One of the more compelling aspects of new monasticism is its interest in contemplative prayer as source and inspiration for the spiritual life. New monastics are discovering the amazing potential of the practice of a rhythm of daily and nightly prayer. Practices such as the praying of the Psalms, rootedness in Scripture, giving space for silence, being at ease with stillness, paying attention to the great garden of creation, and the regular practice of withdrawal, can all be found in the daily experience of various new monastic communities. The hOME community offers 'Stillpoint', a place for meditation in the Christian contemplative tradition; the 'Morning Bell' daily call to prayer sent out by text message and e-mail comes from the Pace Bene project in Oxford; the Moot Community in London offer Prayer Development Days.

An impulse for mission

The monastic friars of the pre-modern world were sent to serve specific localities by providing care and support for the poor and sick. Similarly, new monastics seek to engage in mission to particular localities in the UK and abroad. The Simple Way community in Philadelphia, USA, have deliberately gone to the poorest area of that city, where no other church would go, and set up a profoundly loving and radical community that fights for the rights and welfare of local marginalized people. The Moot Community is currently in negotiation with the Diocese of London to move from the privilege of Westminster and the City of London to an inner-city estate just north of the City, precisely to follow this monastic inclination to serve the economic poor and the spiritually impoverished.

Monastic communities have traditionally been good at moving into new settings, often places where others fear to go, and lovingly engaging with local people. Almost all of them embrace the monastic tradition of offering hospitality to the stranger, traveller or visitor. Concerning mission activities, they actively seek the spiritual in the secular. For example, some provide low-cost evening meals in local cafés followed by a Eucharist. feig, a community based at Gloucester cathedral, have a regular café space aimed at spiritual tourists. The mayBe community take their sacramental life into different city parks throughout the year both as a means of connecting with the wider community and of engaging with the seasons. The Moot Community took over an art gallery for ten days in Lent, using it as a prayer, poetry, art and performance space, enabling spiritual tourists and the de-churched to explore Christianity.

The vision here is about trying to discern and catch up with what God is already doing in and through culture. Rather than fearing contemporary culture, like some churches, new monastics enter the broken and dark places of our society knowing that this is precisely where Christ can be found. They therefore represent a hopeful discourse centred on the love of God, and the graceful action of God in our world, through social and spiritual transformation. Such activity is the consequence of authentic Christian contemplative awareness. As McCarthy writes:

> One becomes more aware and attentive to the realities of everyday life, the struggles and triumphs of very real people in very real circumstances. Authentic spirituality has consequences for life in society; it is concerned with the broken places in our world and is invested in the repair of the world.
> (McCarthy, 1999, p. 200)

A love for the earth

That monasticism encourages a love for the earth and its creatures is a further reason for its attractiveness. Monasteries have always been very good at growing things, both for themselves and the benefit of others. The Franciscans are particularly well known for such endeavours:

> In Francis, there is a divine call to love, embracing both nature and neighbour in a healing and reconciling union that

is the pattern both for ecology and political relationships throughout the world.
(Ramon, 1994, p. 130)

For new monastic groups this is strongly linked to the view that all of life is holy; this is particularly relevant in view of the environmental degradation so widespread in our world today. The online community Earth Abbey describes itself as 'a movement of people helping one another to live more in tune with the earth' and of pursuing a 'life-affirming, creative spirituality'. The monastic terminology used by Earth Abbey is no accident; rather it is evidence of a twenty-first century network-community finding new ways to live through the ancient practices of monasticism.

Insights enabling community life

A key characteristic of the spiritual tourist is the desire to belong relationally in a community, and an equal measure of fear of that belonging.

> One of the most crucial hallmarks of the postmodern situation is what might be called 'the return to relationships' ... Humans are fundamentally social creatures and therefore the emptiness individuals sense can never be filled by the abundance of possessions but only in relationships with others.
> (Grenz, 2003, pp. 252–68)

Many of the new monastic communities are exploring how to develop a depth of relationship that can cope with two new forms of contextual community: the network community where people live apart, and the geographically specific community of those who live near or with each other. The use of a rhythm of life and regular communal events has been the focus for the network side of community. The real challenge begins when we attempt to live nearby or in the same house as each other. The highly individualized culture in which many of us were brought up has meant that few of us acquired the skills necessary for such forms of community; these must be learned by trial and error. Some groups have become aware of the need to function as therapeutic communities, to enable members to learn tolerance and compromise. This is a major challenge of being a community today, and yet Christian community is vital if we are to establish authentic Christian spirituality:

> We do not undertake the spiritual quest alone. We need communities which nurture and hold us, communities which keep traditions and charisms alive and which hand them on to the next generation ... Thus an individual, privatized or purely personal spirituality is an oxymoron. Authentic spirituality can never be an isolated, privatized or an individual affair. It is always located in a particular community from which it derives flavour, character and efficacy.
> (McCarthy, 1999, p. 200)

Many new monastic communities – such as Church of the Apostles in Seattle – have set up community houses that enable a spiritual patterning of life. These provide the benefit of shared monastic living: patterns of work, prayer, worship, rest and action, all of which bring real spiritual depth and vitality to residents and their guests. Living less expensively in shared accommodation frees residents up to give time to activities centred on worship, mission and community. Church of the Apostles has become a success precisely because their community houses have enabled real engagement with the Fremont area of the city, one of the least churched places in the USA.

Similarly, the Moot community in London seeks to take over a large clergy house to set up such an intentional community, which it is hoped will then provide the focus and energy for mission in an inner-city estate. Being and doing intentional community is hard, but it is a crucial strategy for new monastics. Community houses can be the relational powerhouses of loving action and mission – what the friaries and monasteries were to traditional monastics.

In conclusion, and contrary to the opinion of some commentators, the authors contend that fresh expressions of monasticism do not dumb down on the monastic tradition. Rather they wrestle with the need for mission, drawing on an authentic and relevant expression of the Christian faith for our post-secular, post-religious culture of mysticism. New Monastics seek to be faithful to the pre-modern friars and a long line of lay activist and monastic communities (including Dorothy Day and the Catholic Worker Movement), in the creation of radical and contextual expressions of spiritual community. They seek the social and spiritual transformation of local communities through relationship, hospitality and loving service. In fellowship with Benedict and Francis, new monastics seek to build radical communities that are fully integrated into society and the wider Church, working collaboratively wherever possible. As such they continue the development of a living tradition of pioneering, risk-taking mission that draws deeply on a catholic and contemplative tradition that can be traced right back to the desert mothers and fathers.

References

Church of the Apostles, 'About: Values', viewed on 23 December 2008, http://www.apostleschurch.org/about_values.php.

Dorothy Day, 1946, 'On Pilgrimage, 1946', *The Catholic Worker*, Vol. 10.

S. J. Grenz, 2003, 'Ecclesiology', in K. J. Vanhoozer (ed.), 2003, *The Cambridge Companion to Postmodern Theology*, Cambridge: Cambridge University Press.

George Guiver CR, 1990, *Faith in Momentum*, London: SPCK.

Marie McCarthy, 1999, 'Spirituality in a Postmodern Era', in Pattison and Woodward.

maybe, 'Spirit of mayBe', viewed on 23 December 2008, http://www.maybe.org.uk/cms/scripts/page.php?site_id=mb&item_id=values.

Ian J. Mobsby, 2007, *Emerging and Fresh Expressions of Church*, London: Moot Community Publishing.

Ian J. Mobsby, 2008, *The Becoming of G-d*, Cambridge: YTC Press.

St Francis of Assisi, *Little Flowers of St Francis of Assisi*, ch. XI.

Stephen Pattison and J. Woodward (eds), 1999, *A Blackwell Reader in Pastoral and Practical Theology*, Oxford: Blackwell.

Br Ramon SSF, 1994, *Franciscan Spirituality*, London: SPCK.
Br Roger, 2000, *The Sources of Taizé*, London: Continuum.
Safespace, 'Core Principles', viewed on 23 December 2008, http://homepage.mac.com/markjohnberry/safe-space/.
Barry Taylor, 2008, *Entertainment Theology*, Michigan: Baker Academic.
R. S. Thomas, 1995, *Collected Poems 1945–1990*, London: Phoenix.

Note

1 As recorded at the Action and Contemplation Conference, York, 2007.

Acknowledgement

The extract from 'Gift' by R. S. Thomas is in *Collected Poems 1945–1990*, Phoenix, 1995, and is used by permission.

4

Midwifing the
Movement of the Spirit

THOMAS BRACKETT

At 2:00 pm on 23 March 2009, I began a journey of discovery with a remarkable group of leaders in the Church of
England. It started when the Reverend Chris Jones picked me
up at the Liverpool Train Station and invited me to join several
clergy for an afternoon of training. For the next three weeks,
I witnessed the Pioneer Ministries sponsored by the Church
of England's Fresh Expressions agency, the Church Missionary
Society and the Church Army. Via the hospitality of leaders
in three dioceses, I witnessed transformative ministries in five
metropolitan areas, as well as several in more rural areas. During this remarkable tour, I plied nearly everyone I met with a
question: 'If you knew twenty years ago what you know now
about the impact of secularization on the relationship of English culture to the Church of England (and vice versa), how
might you have prepared the institution differently for those
emerging realities?' Most of the leaders I interviewed understood that I was not asking a rhetorical question, that I came
to them eager to explore a perspective that might inform our
leadership in the Episcopal Church. Of the seventy-six people
I queried, I filled a notebook with the highlights of forty-two
conversations.

Here is the gist of what they shared: 'Twenty years ago, we
were unintentionally pushing our young people out the back
doors of our churches—mostly through indifference to the gifts

they tried to offer. The long-term impact of that benign neglect is that we traded a generation of young leaders and artists and prophets for various attempts to maintain the status quo. Today, we are working on bringing new young leaders into our churches, but that's not the same as nurturing the prophetic voice in community—training new leaders to cultivate community with a hoe instead of directing with the verger's mace. That takes time to develop. It's an art of "being in community" that very few have ever experienced, much less mastered.'

I pressed my conversation partners further and asked, 'So then, how would you recommend that we Americans might respond to this hard-earned wisdom you've offered?' Their answers were straightforward: 'Start now—don't wait until you have this all figured out. Experiment joyfully and publicly with new forms of ministry that match the cultures in which you find your ministries. Fail early and fail often until you learn what works. Learn to trust the young prophets in your midst and don't be afraid when the visions they share are out beyond your comfort zones. Be daring and be bold!'

Interspersed with these interviews were visits to ministries on the ground. One of the first ministries I witnessed in the Liverpool area was Oaks Church in Tanhouse, Skelmersdale. Before making any plans, the Reverend Duncan Petty and his wife, Ann, took their time to get to know the community they felt called to serve.[1] They discovered that there was a 'need for building small, relational, supportive, stable groups with some sort of security for people whose lives are all over the place.' Instead of planning a traditional new church launch that gathered the community on Sundays, they felt the call to be a twenty-four-hour-a-day, seven-day-a-week community center of healing that offers hope to this largely unemployed and emotionally struggling community. In their words, they purchased 'through sacrificial giving of ... members plus finance from sending church and elsewhere, a community house for blessing the locals through a variety of small groups.' Ministry in this unique neighborhood called for the service of a house manager and a youth and children's worker for twenty hours a week each.

The diocese pays the rent on their home in the center of the community, and they are as embedded in this intentional community of outreach as a family can be. My time with them repeatedly brought me to joy and gratitude—joy over the incarnational presence they are offering and gratitude for the way they called me to reexamine my understanding of what it means to be a sacramental people.

What might be happening here with the Pettys? What is so different about the shape of this ministry? In Duncan's words, they had to 'leave behind their stereotypical ideas on what it means to offer ministry in community.' I could see clearly that what they were doing was best likened to a kind of spiritual 'midwifing.' They went into the grinding poverty of that housing project to search out what the Spirit is birthing—one could say they walked around their new neighborhood as 'archeologists of hope.'[2] And they pledged to be present to that birth, to honor whatever the Spirit might be bringing to life.

I do recognize the cultural differences between the Church of England and the Episcopal Church, and I am aware that my perspective has been shaped by some very thoughtful leaders both within and outside of our Episcopal Church over the last twenty years. And yet, the Petty's journey is a unique example of what I believe to be the future of midwifing ministry for all of us. I offer in this essay an urgent invitation to the Church to midwife the work of the Spirit in a world longing for reconciliation.

From Hospice Ward to Birthing Center

On my return to the United States, I immediately gathered a group of leaders in the Episcopal Church, as well as staff at the Episcopal Church Center. The point of our six conversations was to explore practical responses to apply what I had learned in the United Kingdom to our US context. These leaders helped me reflect on my day-to-day encounters with both innovative and declining ministries across the Episcopal Church. I began to notice an awakening of sorts among many of our church's leaders. There seems to be a new impatience with the old models of church and church leadership passed to us from the 'inherited church.'³ Many of our church leaders are realizing that, for most of their careers, they have been offering a kind of hospice ministry to their congregations and dioceses. It is not just the flagging attendance and the graying of our denomination's membership that push them to acknowledge the *ennui* of our beloved institutions. It is also the noted absence of fresh visions and dreams that would normally bubble up from our younger members. There seems to be a fresh hunger for the Spirit's promise to give above and beyond 'all we can ask or imagine' (Eph 3:20–21).

At the same time, there are also many leaders who are eager to maintain our structures and habits just a little longer. Many of them left their seminary experiences years ago confident that, if they just offered excellent ministry and relevant preaching, there was hope of reversing the declining trends, at least on a local level. Today, they faithfully and persistently make up for declining offerings and pledges by working harder and longer towards a balanced budget and for their stipends. Their best-attended services seem to be those remembering the good old days—the High Holy Golden Days of the Church of Yesterday. There are others who are convinced that only a return to orthodoxy will secure God's blessings on our ecclesiastical ventures.

It is not so difficult to understand how the Church arrived at this state of affairs. Even today, most of our seminarians are trained to coordinate the ministries of churches whose identities were cast in a pre-modern era, the earliest days of Christendom. (By 'Christendom' I refer to the offspring produced by the official marriage of the early Christian movement to the Roman Empire.) Furthermore, most of our mainline denominations were assembled on a theological framework cobbled together at a time when the Church's authority was granted by the state and the Church operated from the center of society. In those halcyon days, the leaders of our churches were seen as the keepers of all that is good and whole and godly. It was their calling to bring God to the world—to introduce the Christian life to the 'lost' out there. The world changed, but the calling has yet to be recast. And so, many leaders find themselves engaged in hospice care for denominations and churches in their latter days.

Rest assured, I am convinced that hospice ministry to declining congregations is desperately needed today. It is a challenging and significant ministry, primarily because it calls us to face our own mortality, as well as our (as yet unredeemed) addictions to certainty and ensured outcomes. We all want to think of ourselves as resurrection people. Sadly, many of us are so eager to arrive at Easter morning that we skip over the trauma of Good Friday—primarily because we dare not look into the face of death, especially the death of our church, our diocese or our denomination.

Friends of mine who make a living as hospice chaplains tell me that, when a patient dies, the most difficult family member to engage is the one who hid away from most of the patient's dying process, acting as though their loved one would eventually get better. Though perhaps not in such a morbid way, I believe many of our theologians and church leaders struggle with that same urge. It is simply easier to turn away from the death and dying process in our midst, to pretend we are still at the center of society and that the world still cares deeply about our educated opinion. The alternative—facing the loss of roles that once defined us, loss of control, loss of what might have been—is too much to bear.

For this reason, compassionate, loving and respectful hospice ministry for our churches is essential. In particular, those who care for parishes in long-term decline point out that institutions struggling with their own death and dying process exhibit a strong need for routine, predictability, and a controlled environment. It is important to tell the 'right' story—to preserve the sacred memories of the parish in its golden days and to maintain their structures. As a result, a key offering of this ecclesiastical hospice ministry is to appreciatively celebrate and preserve memories of the community at its best. In fact, faith communities (and even denominations) in this stage of their life cycle will often choose to carefully archive their memories, rather than creating new high points in their life together. One of the leader's roles is to graciously and kindly midwife the community from the life they have loved into that community's next life.

One may wonder why I have devoted such attention to this hospice ministry, when ultimately my reflections are offered for those who feel the Spirit's call to midwife fresh expressions of all that She is birthing into our world. The two ministries often live side by side. In fact, birthing new ministries that emerge from within the inherited church could be likened to setting up a birthing center in the middle of a hospice ward. Some of the more powerful examples of this reality can be found in the homeless ministries sponsored within Episcopal churches. For the lack of funding and their own worship space, many of these fledgling ministries set up their services in the undercrofts of our downtown parishes, where there is public transportation available and accessibility for people with disabilities. As the more formal service upstairs is going out in peace to love and serve the Lord, helpers downstairs are setting up chairs in circles, with a table of fellowship in the center and musicians getting ready to lead worship with music from Africa, from the Caribbean, and from God-loving musicians who live on the street. Many are surprised to see folks who used to attend the earlier 'upstairs' service. They now come to the later downstairs service because they also sense that the Spirit is birthing something new.

On any given Sunday, life for these upstairs/downstairs communities can get chaotic. Nicely dressed churchgoers on their way out may encounter musicians rehearsing more earthy and soulful music in the parish garden. Some of those musicians may be homeless; some are professionals grateful for the opportunity to come alongside a ministry that invites them to get real with issues seldom addressed in our more refined Sunday services. It is that sort of 'mixing it up' that a birthing center in a hospice ward may require.

I was recently asked, 'Do you think that it is possible or

advisable to open such a birthing clinic in the center of our hospice ward?' My answer is, 'It depends.' I think it depends on whether we can take responsibility for our real motives for tackling such a challenge. As many observers can attest, it produces a nasty case of cognitive dissonance when an emergent church planter claims to be midwifing new ministries of the Spirit, but their real motivation is to keep our denomination from dying by starting new churches with good form. At that moment our institutional narcissism emerges from the underbrush of our own marketing. With all my heart I believe that keeping the denomination alive is one ministry and midwifing the emerging work of the Spirit is another. Much of the time, we struggle to stay clear about the difference between the two.

Here, then, is the rub. It may be that many of us are trying to offer a midwife's presence in the Spirit's birthing clinic (the whole world), even as we are guided by hospice theology and Christendom practices. In other words, we get excited about the new work of the Spirit in God's world, and then we try to bring it back to church so that we can label it, own it and civilize it to match our culture. As a result, we may be missing the incredible beauty of our call to midwife the work of the Spirit in a world longing for reconciliation with God, humanity and all of creation.

Right now, I believe the Spirit is birthing aspects of the future that She has longed to make known from before time. I also sense that the Spirit longs for partners in that holy process of making all things new. Our highest calling may be to discover, midwife and then celebrate all that the Spirit is birthing in our midst as well as out there in the world. To take this new model for ministry seriously, though, we must face some daunting challenges.

Challenge #1: Make the transition from leaders prized for institutional expertise to leaders skilled in midwifing new forms of ministry

One trainer of midwives explained to me that, by the very nature of their work, midwives offer a covenant for *presence*, that is, they commit to being fully present to the one giving birth, to that which is being birthed, as well as to the actual birthing process. This wise woman impressed on me that the midwife cannot offer any guarantees, only a covenant. This is also a covenant for *purpose*: to offer every resource available for the sake of a complete birthing process. Finally, in her own words, the trainer insisted that this is also a covenant between the midwife and the whole family to fully participate in whatever happens.

Speaking practically, when an experienced midwife walks in to work with a mother about to give birth that day, her initial concerns are around some very specific issues. She asks the mother about the timing of her contractions. Her sensors are discerning the suitability of the environment, the supportiveness of the family, the mother's mood and whether or not the baby about to come into this world is experiencing distress. In other words, she is pacing the process of this delivery and coming alongside. Unlike some of the busy doctors in our large hospitals, most midwives can afford to let the mother's process set the pace of their interactions. This is an incredible model for new ministry today. If we were to adopt this way of being in the world—if we were to take on the role of midwife to the Spirit—we might be called to move into unfamiliar environments to sense exactly what it is that the Spirit might be birthing out there.

Would it not make a tremendous difference if we were to train our church leaders in the art and science of midwifery, as well as everything else we think they need to know? Imagine if we asked our clergy to consider the high calling of midwifing that which the Spirit is birthing in their respective communities? To speak of ourselves as incarnational communities would take on a whole new meaning. Instead of our rice paper communion wafers held up as the ultimate symbol of God's presence, 'that which is being birthed' might call us to prepare a sumptuous meal intentionally shared with strangers-now-guests. We might even hold up the stories of the Spirit's in-breaking presence outside of church as evidence of Emmanuel, proof that 'God is with us.' Such a shift would ask us to consider story-listening as an advanced level of evangelism—listening for evidence that God is at work, that the Spirit is birthing new life, that God is alive and well.

It is this very sort of evangelism that set up the birthing station known to many around the world as 'Common Cathedral.'[4] When Debbie Little-Wyman encountered people of the street loitering around the steps of the Cathedral Church of St Paul in Boston in the 1990s, she eventually sat down next to them and listened deeply to their stories of hope and for signs of grace. Eventually, Debbie realized that not only was there a growing number of homeless people eager to join a community of faith, she also realized that she was being called to midwife that emerging reality.

It was initially a stretch for church leaders to recognize Debbie's call to the priesthood or to see her gathering at a fountain on Boston Common as a viable congregation. Little did she know it, but Debbie was actually midwifing a ministry that would eventually become the birthing station for dozens more street ministries around the world. Today, when seminarians from various denominations visit her 'Come and See' weekends to learn the nuts and bolts of this birthing station ministry, it is common to hear remarks like, 'I only wish that this is what I was learning in seminary, right now.'

The Church would be a different place if our seminaries taught these skills of community organizing, deep listening, transformational interviewing and action/inquiry. Within a generation, we might value birthing stations like the one Debbie Little-Wyman and Duncan and Ann Petty and many others have created every bit as much as our fine Cathedral ministries.

Challenge #2: Get over the assumption that 'emergent' and 'fresh' are all about us

Recently during a church conference, a colleague asked me, 'What do you think is emerging, Tom?' At that very moment, the building's fire alarm went off. While we were shuffling out to the safe zone, I helped a very pregnant woman down the steps. As we reached the parking lot, it occurred to me that, if we were to ask her, 'What is emerging, Helen?' she might say, 'Are you asking, "Is my baby going to be a boy or a girl?"' In her experience, the word 'emerging' refers to a process pointedly different from the way we banter the term about. She is clear that she is not emerging. Her doctor is not emerging. Her midwife is not emerging. In fact, it is the baby that is emerging. Yet, when it comes to our theological conversations, we like to think it is Mother Church that is somehow crowning and emerging. In other words, we would like to think it is all about us.

When we say emerging or emergent or emergence church, most of us tend to think that what is emerging is a new variation of Christendom or some new expression of church. In fact, based on my recent review of exactly 146 articles and essays in journals concerned with congregational development here in the US, I find an alarming incidence of church leaders and academics writing about 'emerging church' as a means of revitalizing congregations in decline. The general outline of their argument goes something like this: We live in a changing world and the way to get young people to come to church is to try out new worship or new outreach (or maybe some combination of vintage worship and e-reach).

The strategy is highly problematic, because once again the inherited church is at the center. Please know that, if I sound critical of Christendom, it is because I am. By and large, Christendom is best at forming self-absorbed groups that foster anxious instincts around institutional self-preservation. We think we already know what it is the world needs from us, and we spend our time creating strategic plans to make that happen.

Even Duncan Petty admits, 'It is so easy to ... run away with your initiatives instead of looking for what the Spirit is up to and going with that. We have, for example, just because we did it in more conventional settings, tried to run basics courses. . . before people were ready for them, and they duly flopped.'[5] More and more of us are convinced that the Spirit is calling us to repent of the urge to impose our expectations on the Spirit's work. The Oaks Church in England may never be self-sustaining and it may never reach parish status or fit limited definitions of a conventional church. At the same time, ministries like this deserve our finest leaders, our generous support and a fresh reverence for their capacity to transform all of us.

Challenge #3: Get comfortable with working 'out of bounds'

A few years ago I came across this quote from Jürgen Moltmann:

> Mission is not primarily an activity of the church, but an attribute of God. God is a missionary God. It is not the Church that has a mission of salvation to fulfill in the world; it is the mission of the Son and the Spirit through the Father that includes the Church. There is church because there is mission, not vice versa. The Church must not think its role is identical to the *missio Dei*; the Church is participating in the mission of God. The Church's mission is a subset of a larger whole mission. That is, it is part of God's mission to the world and not the entirety of God's work in the world. (Moltmann, p. 64)

Moltmann's words are challenging to many of our leaders, lay and ordained. He is claiming that we do not have the franchising rights to God's movement in the world. This also means that if we are to partner with God, we *must* give up the need to own what it is that God is birthing. On reflection, it seems as though followers of Jesus Christ have always struggled with the need to 'brand' with our own logo whatever the Spirit is birthing. This has been a perennial issue for our established denominations.

With this in mind, the inclusion of the Acts of the Apostles in the Christian canon may actually be a great act of editorial compassion. We might think of this as a record of the first church's bungled opportunities, fear, public feuds and failures—all logged for the encouragement and consolation of every follower of Jesus Christ since those early years. The Acts record is full of examples of church leaders struggling to accept the Spirit's ministry beyond their preservation mentality. This is most assuredly a record of the Spirit's generosity—an overwhelming outpouring of divine love on all. It is also the record of a community that finally understood what it means to empty ourselves of our preconceived notions so that we might take on the form of the servant.[6]

There is also an unsettling aspect to the Gospel records of Jesus' teachings and practices. Over and over, we read stories in which Jesus' passionate spirituality trumps the dominant religious traditions of his world. The new communities that were birthed from Jesus' followers had to burst through the restraints of their cultural and religious womb. They were often birthed by the Spirit with midwives who could not understand what it was they were witnessing. They expected God to show up in ways with which they were already comfortable, and God rarely obliged.

On my computer screensaver, I have a remarkable photograph I found online. The image is a picture of a moist mushroom pushing its way up through a thick patch of asphalt—unharmed. All around the emerging fungus are broken pieces of that stretch of parking lot, scattered like a jack hammer had torn them apart. Most people are incredulous when they first see the photo. From a spore buried under asphalt is birthed something so powerful that it can break up the very paths we create for ourselves. The question is, where might we see this happening in our churches today?

In the Acts 15 record of the Spirit's birthing of a new faith community, those most reluctant to receive all that the Spirit offered were the insiders. We might even say their sacred cultural norms were the asphalt that the Spirit had to break up. The metaphor has its limits, but I believe it illuminates the challenges the established Church faces when the Spirit asks us to cast our nets from the 'wrong' side of the boat.

Challenge #4: Let go of our insistence on conformity

The idea of midwifing the work of the Spirit may seem more comfortable now. You might even be a church planter starting out on your first walkabout to explore exactly what God might be doing in your new neighborhood. You commit yourself to openness and a genuine sense of curiosity. You pack up your clipboard and camera and head out into your world to spot what it is that you may be called to midwife. As you walk down Main Street in your neighborhood, a question occurs to you: 'Might it be that the Spirit arrived here before I did?' After that initial query, others follow: 'What kind of work might the Spirit have been doing in this community, prior to the arrival of my church planting initiative? Might it be that God was out here reconciling the world to himself before there were any church-sponsored faith formation classes or evangelism or discipleship going on? How, then, might I come alongside and simply be present to and then celebrate the Spirit's work?'

A key step in that direction would be to acknowledge that all theology is, in reality, indigenous. That is, theology springs up from the community in which it is experienced. It is formed in community and tested in relationship. In fact, we might say that theology, outside of philosophical pursuits, is relationship language—language that reflects the relationship of the individual and the community to the divine. If we take that claim to heart, we might loosen our ecclesiastical control mechanisms enough to make space for a community to design and lead worship and construct an organizational life that matches their culture and their theology.

Consider the following example of what such a process might

look like in practice. Recently, I was contacted by a community organizer who had served on her diocese's Executive Council for two terms. She and a team of friends had identified a neighborhood with particular unmet needs and had pooled their financial resources to start an after-school drop-in program for Latino and Hispanic children, as well as a weekend club for the Asian youth in the area. They opened their doors two-and-a-half years ago and now have an average of 130 families attending their weekly parenting classes.

Recently they asked the parents, one by one, whether there was interest in starting a worship gathering based on the Book of Common Prayer but shaped by the community's creative responses to the Spirit's work in their midst. With the exception of two families, the response was an enthusiastic 'Yes!' For the last eight months, they have gathered. They start each of their service planning sessions with the sharing of a meal and samples of people's favorite spiritual music playing in the background. They then share stories of encounters with God at work in the world, and then explore participants' best experiences with God, identifying common themes that consistently emerge. The evening session ends with prayers offered by the participants, often written for that evening's gatherings.

This team of service planners has named their goal as 'the creation of indigenous ritual that honors an Anglican way of being in the world by adhering to the shape of the Book of Common Prayer's forms for worship.' Everyone has always been welcome to attend and participate in this process. They are now gathering commitments for a 'First Sunday in Advent' launch date for this new worshipping community. The community leaders set the goal of having 250 people attend their first service. During the prayers of the people, they will show video clips of stories from those present—stories of the ways they have encountered God in their everyday lives. They are planning to have translators for three languages in each of their services.

But then comes the risk. Recently, the two co-leaders approached their diocesan leaders with a rather novel request. They asked the bishop to help them find a priest who would contract with them to fulfill a priest's sacerdotal responsibilities in their weekly service, and no more. They specifically requested a priest who would honor the order of service as the community had planned it (and as the bishop had pre-approved it). They will handle all of the other pastoral care responsibilities with lay leaders trained via the Diocesan School of Ministry. The priest will be 'called' permanently, though contracted six months at a time and paid weekly for his or her Sunday ministry. The rest of the ministry will be managed by non-ordained leaders, primarily on a volunteer basis. They are still waiting to find that priest.

This is one of the more exciting examples of a creative response to a community's real needs. It also offers a model of ministry midwifery where the priest is a member of the team, but not necessarily the leader. If we can let go of the need for conformity, indigenous ministries like this one could truly flourish.

Closing reflections

In the six months that have passed since my visit to the UK, I have spent hours and hours interviewing lay and ordained leaders in the Episcopal Church on video. My question has been: 'How do you "smell" God at work?', which quickly becomes, 'How have you learned to recognize when it is God at work that you are witnessing?' The answers have been breathtaking. It takes only a slight shift in attention to move to the question on which this essay has focused: 'How have you learned to come alongside and bless the new life that the Spirit is birthing in the world around you?' After a few minutes of this heart-to-heart conversation, I often hear these words: 'Why can't I make this midwifing ministry my everyday calling?' That question is music to my ears.

Have you heard the Spirit's call to distance yourself from hospice ministry, incredible and noble calling that it is? Do you wake up in the night with a longing to return to your first love for ministry, to glimpses of God's daring hopes for all of us? It may well be time to head to the Spirit's birthing center, because I believe now, more than ever, God's dreams are longing to be birthed here in our midst. All that the Spirit quietly asks of you today is that you say 'Yes' to God's hopes emerging.

Reference

Jürgen Moltmann, 1977, *The Church in the Power of the Spirit: A Contribution to Messianic Ecclesiology*, London: SCM Press.

Notes

1 The ministry is referred to as Oaks Church in Tanhouse, Skelmersdale. More information can be found here: https://lccsecure.lancashire. gov.uk/ACS/findExtOrg/view/details.asp?intServiceID=504.

2 This is a metaphor used extensively to explain a way of being called for in the practice of Narrative Therapy. For more on this topic, see Gerald Monk, 1997, *Narrative Therapy in Practice: The Archaeology of Hope*, San Francisco: Jossey-Bass.

3 This is a term used in the 'Mission-shaped Church' report issued by the Archbishop's Council in the Church of England. A downloadable version can be found at www.cofe.anglican.org/info/papers/mission_shaped_church.pdf.

4 For more information, consult Common Cathedral's website: http://www.ecclesia-ministries.org.

5 For more information, read Duncan and Ann Petty's reflections: http://www.sharetheguide.org/comment2.

6 Otto Scharmer's *Theory U* offers fresh perspective on what this kenotic process might look like through the lens of a Process Consulting approach to organizational transformation. This is a very thoughtful approach to moving past 'downloading' old habits onto new possibilities. See Otto Scharmer, 2009, *Theory U: Leading from the Future as It Emerges*, San Francisco: Berrett-Kohler.

5

Letting Your Actions Do the Talking: Mission and the Catholic Tradition

BISHOP STEPHEN COTTRELL

Many people today are uneasy about the slums, but it is too often an uneasiness produced by fear. It is not more policemen who are wanted in places like Battersea and Somers Town: it is God Incarnate in the hearts of loving human beings. (Ingram, 1936, p. 6)

So said Father Basil Jellicoe, Assistant Priest of St Mary's, Somers Town, in 1924. Somers Town was a slum parish at the back of Euston Station and it was in that year that he and some associates formed the St Pancras House Improvement Society, pledging to renovate and rebuild the slums in their area. Under Jellicoe's direction flats were built, houses were bought and re-conditioned; nursery schools and savings clubs were started. And controversially, in the interests of providing some alternative entertainment for his impoverished parishioners, Jellicoe opened what he called a 'reformed pub'. 'The Anchor' was opened in 1929 and the Archbishop of Canterbury and the Prince of Wales were amongst its first customers (Ingram, 1936, pp. 78–9). The 'Parson running a Pub' story ran in all the newspapers, giving publicity not only to this inventive ministry but also to the whole work of slum clearance and the terrible condition in which many people lived. It is a story to rival the most innovative of today's pioneering ministries or fresh expressions. It reminds us that there is nothing new under the sun; that the whole history of Christian mission has been a history of innovation and fresh expression. As the Church encounters new cultures and new challenges it seeks to serve the needs of ordinary people and give expression to the gospel in a language they understand: something that meets them where they are and takes them somewhere else.

Although Basil Jellicoe is undoubtedly one of the most flamboyant and remarkable of the Anglo-Catholic slum priests of the late Victorian and early twentieth-century period, his story is by no means an isolated one. Behind the example of Jellicoe stand many other priests who built churches in the heart of the slums, and brought colour and beauty to worship in ways that gave a genuine and liberating fresh expression to church life. Such ministries lifted people out of the squalor of their surroundings and gave them the worth and dignity they had been denied almost everywhere else.

Father Lincoln Wainright served in St Peter's Church at the London Docks for 56 years. Building on the legacy of his illustrious predecessor, Father Charles Lowder, he raised money for the church and for the development and maintenance of many schools. When writing to wealthy benefactors he would often speak of the 'salubrious air' of Gravel Lane and he would encourage them to holiday in Wapping: 'If you need a change of air, I can't imagine why you don't try the air here!' (Menzies, 1947, p. 21).

The Fresh Expressions movement has been a breath of fresh air in the twenty-first century Church. However, it has not always been a movement that those from a catholic tradition within the Church of England, or indeed catholic Christians from other churches and traditions, have felt entirely comfortable with. Of course there are exceptions to this, but many priests and parishes have felt anxious that a mission-shaped church has actually turned out to be a church-shaped mission (Hull, 2006), with some of the vital elements of a truly catholic witness (especially a bias to the poor and a challenging of unjust structures) giving way to a kind of ecclesiastical niche marketing where churches are tailored to meet the needs of a particular group. The very word 'catholic' means universal: something that is for everyone. Therefore there has been understandable reluctance to embrace a movement that seems either to label everything 'church' (the worst bit of fresh expressions has been the re-branding of every parent and toddler group in the country as a fresh expression of church), or endlessly split people into coalitions of the like-minded, each with their own service to go to! Moreover, some of the keenest exponents of fresh expressions have also expounded a theology that overemphasized the so-called individual relationship with Christ over and against the corporate, incarnational and sacramental belonging to Christ within his body the Church – the bedrock of catholic ecclesiology.

So how do fresh expressions fit into the catholic tradition of mission and service? I have five starting points that I hope will enable catholic Christians to think their way into the challenge of becoming a 'mixed economy' church and to see how fresh expressions make sense within the catholic tradition: the eight o'clock Mass as it is still celebrated in many churches on virtually every Sunday morning; the actual needs and desires of the people who live in the parish; the dedication festival; the weekday Mass; and finally that group of people with whom the church has real contact but who have never really got involved in its worshipping life.

Understanding the mixed economy church: the eight o'clock!

Quite simply, if you have an eight o'clock Mass in your church on a Sunday morning you have already crossed a theological Rubicon by acknowledging (albeit subconsciously) that it is appropriate for there to be *two* distinct worshipping communities meeting in the same building on a Sunday morning. Although there are some people who come to the eight o'clock because they can't make it to the so-called 'main celebration' later on, we all know that for most of the congregation this *is* the main celebration. They never come to anything else. If, from a catholic perspective, one of the principled objections to fresh expressions is that we should be doing all that we can to draw people together around the *one* table of the Lord, then it follows that we should really cancel the eight o'clock. This is what a few churches have done. But most of us persist with this theological anomaly because we know that it meets the needs of a particular group of people who like and support a particular style of worship. These are people who for all sorts of reasons (good and bad!) don't want the noise, bustle, length and style of what is on offer later in the morning. So the eight o'clock remains. Ironically, this most conservative of services points beyond itself to a theological rationale for a different way of ordering all the worship of the local church. If it's appropriate to have two distinct worshipping communities, why not three or four? This is the beginning of what is meant by a 'mixed economy' church, a phrase used by Archbishop Rowan Williams in support of the whole development of Fresh Expressions (Williams, 2004, p. 5). As Bishop Steven Croft has written, 'There is now broad acceptance across the Church of England ... that we need fresh expressions of church alongside existing and traditional churches' (2008, p. 1). For it is not just questions of timing and style that prevent some people from becoming part of Sunday morning church (whatever the tradition), there are a whole host of other cultural questions and constraints that the Church must reflect upon, and adapt to. Many people work on Sundays. In our rapidly changing context, where no single culture dominates, most people have little knowledge of the Church or the Christian tradition. The Church has always understood that it is necessary to translate the gospel into the language of the people, but now we live in a society where there are many different languages and a mosaic of cultures. It has never been likely that one size will fit all; it is ludicrous to even consider this might be the case in today's world.

Mission-shaped and kingdom focused:[1] serving the
community and participating in the mission of God.

The needs of the world are the *raison d'être* of the Church. In
Anglican ecclesiology, a mission-shaped church is marked by
five characteristics:

- Proclamation of the Good news of the Kingdom
- Teaching, baptizing and nurturing new believers
- Responding to human needs in loving service
- Seeking to transform the unjust structures of society
- Striving to safeguard the integrity of creation, and the sustenance and renewal of the life of the earth.[2]

Mission, therefore, can never be reduced to proclamation; it
overflows into discipleship. It begins with our longing to share
with others all that we have received in Christ, but it cannot
end with initiation. It is initiation *into* the kingdom of God,
which is the eschatological vision that longs to see the world
reordered according to the purposes of God. Hence the missionary church is the church that participates in God's mission,
by enabling all people to become disciples of Christ. And by
disciples I mean people who work toward the building of God's
kingdom by responding to human need in loving service, and
seek to transform the unjust structures of society. Therefore,
the first task of a mission-shaped church is to ask how it can
serve and be a blessing to its local community. Now we see
the relevance of the Anglo-Catholic slum priests whose witness I described at the beginning of this chapter. Although they
are sometimes remembered as the 'ritualists' because of the
troubles they got into by pushing the liturgical envelope further than had been the case before, it is impossible to understand their witness without drawing together the two sides of
this ministry. They gave fresh expression to Anglican liturgy,
renewing its catholic and sacramental character, *and* they
worked to eradicate the poverty they encountered in their parishes, thereby transforming the physical environment in which
they ministered. It was a thoroughgoing sacramental ministry.

Indeed, one could say that it makes no sense without a sacramental understanding of the Christian faith. They believed in transformation. Before Basil Jellicoe embarked upon his great work of developing the St Pancras House Improvement Society, he spent a day in prayer before the blessed sacrament at Pusey House in Oxford. He believed that the bread that is placed upon the altar at the offertory is transformed, and becomes for us the bread of heaven. Likewise, these slum priests believed that any physical part of God's creation could be transformed, that it was capable of bearing the values of the kingdom of God. Indeed, they took their lead from Pusey, who – of all the founding fathers of the Oxford Movement – most emphasized the social nature of the gospel. He wrote that: 'We need missions among the poor of our towns, organized bodies of clergy living among them; licensed preachers in the streets and lanes of our cities' (Peck, 1933, p. 64).

The need is the same today. Our mission begins by listening for the cry of the poor and outcast on our own doorstep. As William Temple (later the Archbishop of Canterbury) asked, preaching in 1919 on Matthew 25, 'Of what avail is it that I glorify [Christ] in his sanctuary or adore him in the blessed sacrament, if when I meet him in the street I turn away from him?'[3]

Mapping the family tree: the dedication festival

When I was serving as Missioner in the Wakefield diocese I gave a talk to a group of clergy – many of whom I knew quite well – about church planting. This was back in the 1990s when the phrase 'fresh expression' had not yet been dreamed up. But it was at a time when the church-planting movement, which did so much to prepare the way for fresh expressions, was challenging the Church to think about how it could establish new worshipping communities, particularly in unchurched neighbourhoods and networks. One priest who was present at the meeting adopted a slightly cynical manner to the whole 'new ways of being church' agenda. He wanted to know why we were bothering with all of this when there was still plenty of life left in old ways of being church and still plenty to do. Having quite a good idea about the church where he served I casually responded by asking him when his church was first built. Marching into the trap, he proudly told the assembled gathering that they had celebrated their 150th anniversary the previous year. Like so many churches in urban West Yorkshire they were established during Victorian times. 'So you're running a church plant?' I suggested with a smile. The penny dropped: every church was planted at some point. Every church owed its existence to the dedicated ministry of a particular group of Christians at a particular time who were seeking to respond to the needs and challenges of their day by establishing some new expression of Christian life. Even if today many of us still are constrained by preconceived notions of what a church ought to be and ought to look like, we need to constantly remind ourselves – to borrow a favourite metaphor of Rowan Williams – that the Church is something that happens before it is something that is institutionally organized: 'It happens when the Good News summons [and] assembles people around Jesus Christ' (Croft, 2008, p. 6). In another address he puts it like this: 'The church is the assembly of those who are finding their lives transfigured by the presence of Jesus' (Williams, 2004, p. 2).

It is therefore helpful for us to remember that the particular branch of the catholic Church, the particular worshipping community we are part of, whatever pattern or shape it now takes, had a beginning that was born of mission. The transfiguring and transforming presence of Jesus compelled men and women in a particular place at a particular time, to give expression to their belonging to Christ and their allegiance to his mission by establishing a church; an outpost in time and space of that constant calling into community of the whole created order – and especially of all humanity. Or, to put it more simply: every old way of being church was once new (Cottrell and Sledge, n.d.). And every new way of being church must become old and in turn give birth to what will follow as the Church responds faithfully to the commission of Christ to proclaim the faith afresh.

The weekday Mass: a fresh expression waiting to happen

I have always served in parishes where there has been daily Mass. On the one occasion when this was not the case, I made establishing it a top priority, because I have always seen daily Mass as the indispensable foundation upon which all other ministries are built. However, if I am honest, I think I had a rather narrow understanding of the Mass in general. I tended to see the Sunday Eucharist as the central point to which everything else flowed, whereas the weekday Eucharist (however valuable) was devotional extra. It was where I and other committed (and available!) members of the congregation could establish a daily rhythm of offering and prayer that would sustain our ministry. In this sense it was seen as a kind of 'topping-up' place for the super spiritual who have already experienced and received a complete expression of church on Sunday. Or, if new people did attend, the task was to guide them somewhere else. But if what I said earlier about the mixed economy of church is right, then every Eucharist has the capacity to be the full expression, that place where all scattered humanity can be welcomed and nurtured.

My own eureka moment came as a parish priest, when I found that several people started coming to a weekday Eucharist who for all sorts of good reasons were never likely to come on Sunday. The competing demands of work and family made it virtually impossible. I had to accept the fact that a Wednesday morning Eucharist was going to be the only church that these people ever came to. Therefore I had to stop seeing it as a staging post and ensure that those who came would find in it a complete expression of church that included the teaching and fellowship one would expect to find on Sunday morning.

I have since discovered that virtually every church that puts on some sort of regular weekday worship finds that people attend who never come on Sunday. We shouldn't be surprised by this: the nature of Sunday has changed massively. What we should be surprised by is the great number of churches who never put on weekday worship at all. And too often those that do, fail to cater, let alone reach out, to those who are not yet Christians or for whom this expression of church will be their only one. Catholic Christians have a real advantage here. Daily worship, especially the Eucharist, has always been part of our tradition. It provides an obvious, natural and easy way to offer alternative possibilities for Christian community and worship. Often this only means re-thinking what is already on offer. In my experience, by simply paying more attention to the preaching, making sure that there is always some music and singing, providing coffee, and perhaps a discussion group after the Mass, the Wednesday morning Eucharist more than doubles in size.

I have used the phrase a 'complete expression of church', and it needs a little explanation. Of course no human expression of church life can be complete in the sense that there is nothing else to know or receive. Missional worship will always have about it those elements of journeying which mean that there is clearly and obviously still more to come. What I mean by 'complete' is that the liturgy should contain those elements of welcome, nurture, hospitality, teaching and sacramental ministry that should be the norm whenever the Christian community happens to gather. However, these elements can be absent if we only see that service as a devotional extra for people who received those things on Sunday and therefore don't necessarily need them on Wednesday. This is another Rubicon to cross, but it opens a door of opportunity at a point in our liturgical life where something we are already offering realizes its missional potential.

A mission-shaped church: starting where people are

Perhaps the greatest account of mission theology in the past twenty years or so is Vincent Donovan's *Christianity Rediscovered*. As a relatively inexperienced Roman Catholic priest posted to East Africa, where many traditional methods of evangelization had not born fruit, Donovan sought to become part of the community and do nothing more than tell the gospel story in the language of the culture, and watch to see if it would take root. This is one of the most interesting worked examples of church as the consequence of the story of God's love taking root and bearing fruit in human culture. The gospel impacted the culture and was allowed to flourish and grow within the language of that culture. Having, as it were, sown the seed, Donovan leaves and allows what happens as a result of the encounter with Christ to take its own shape.

Every expression of church is, in its own way, another worked example of what the encounter with Christ looks like in the life of a particular community. Inevitably, certain expressions of church have come to dominate. This is chiefly because their way of expressing and nurturing faith has proved to be effective and has stood the test of time. It is not part of the Fresh Expressions agenda to either lose sight of this or in any way to undermine it. We need old ways of being church as well as new ones! An honest recognition is required, that one size does not fit all, and that every expression of church is just that, an expression: a certain form and shape that is part of a community's ongoing response to Christ. New cultures and new questions demand new shapes and new responses. Whenever the gospel encounters a new culture it also carries with it the challenge that that church must take on a new expression. It is this recognition, more than anything else, which is the vital first principle of the missiology that has been encouraged by the Fresh Expressions movement.

For catholic Christians, part of this will always be the fresh expression of our sacramental life. But this is something we should not apologise for. On the contrary, we should be provoking the rest of the church into understanding that the sacraments are not a particular cultural expression that can be left behind if wished, but are part of the very fabric of that first encounter. Christ himself is the sacrament of God, and the Church by its nature – not just its cultural expression – is a sacramental community. But it will take different shapes as the gospel encounters new people and new questions. Therefore, the principle we see at work in Vincent Donovan's inspiring ministry to the Masai in East Africa, must be the same as the gospel encounters of the people of East Oxford, East London or the East Midlands. We start by creating some common ground where we can sit down and learn the language and culture of the people we are seeking to serve; listen to their questions; understand their concerns; and then begin to share with them the story of Christ. As we serve, listen and proclaim, so the possibility of church is born: a community formed by the impact of the story of Christ and the witness of his church.

In my own work of encouraging evangelism in the Church, I have often invited churches to base their evangelistic strategy around this question:

How can we serve the people with whom we have contact in such a way that the gospel is intriguing, challenging and appealing?
(Cottrell, 2006, p. 63)

I usually see this question as leading towards some sort of mission or evangelistic event where the church community gets alongside the local community – people it already knows – and speaks somehow to the issues and concerns the community faces. This is a mission principle inspired by Jesus' example on the Emmaus Road. He came alongside those whose lives were going in the wrong direction, but before speaking to them he first asked what they were discussing (Luke 24.17). We come alongside people in a similar way: we build community, listen patiently, open up areas of common concern, build coalitions. Soon we arrive at a point where questions are asked and doors of opportunity opened so that we can begin to share the story of Christ. This same question is also at the heart of Fresh Expressions. As a community of people gather around a particular cause or concern, what is formed is not merely a stepping-stone to church on Sunday, but church itself.

I think there is a great potential within the ordinary day-to-day stuff of ministry for such communities to come together. In the past we have often only seen these as stepping-stones – and there is nothing wrong with this – but some of them could potentially grow if we intentionally saw them as 'church waiting to happen'. The crucial step will probably be the sacramental one. It is when someone from this community seeks baptism that we are most likely to face the question: is this church the place where they should be baptized? If it is to be that place then that community has become a fresh expression of Christian community, the place not only where people receive the Christian faith but where they are initiated into the sacramental life of the Church and grow in their apostolic identity.

We need more of this sort of church and of this sort of intentional evangelization. The catholic movement transformed the Church of England in its first generation because of its theological and spiritual witness to neglected truths about our identity as a church; it transformed the Church of England in its second generation through its missionary zeal, of which astonishing priests like Lowder, Wainright and Jellicoe are great examples. The true defining mark of any authentic movement for renewal is evangelism: we are compelled to share with others the good news we have received. What we have been given is for others, not just ourselves. It is a vision for the renewal of the world not just the security of the Church. Such a theological, spiritual and missiological renewal is needed again from catholic Christians in the Church of England who have for too long found themselves over-occupied with other matters. There are people in our communities asking questions of meaning; tired of the half-baked promises of the world; troubled by the harsh certainties of fundamentalism; and looking for spaces where questions can be addressed and the possibility of God encountered. There is also huge intellectual, spiritual and material need in our nation and in our world; catholic Christianity has something vital to offer. We believe that worship converts. We believe that the presence of Christ is available to us through the sacramental life. Our theology and our witness have inspired some of the world's greatest music, poetry and art and they continue to inspire today. But we do need to learn some new languages so that they can inspire again and so that the impact of Christ can form new communities of faith. If we are true to the roots of our renewal within the Church of England, and more importantly to the missiological lessons that we see worked out in the New Testament itself, then we must be prepared to cross new frontiers, learn new languages, allow some things to die and others to thrive. The fresh expressions of church that emerge will be true to our inheritance of faith in ways that will both comfort and amaze. Any fresh expression of church must be continuous with the past: the catholic faith must always be 'that faith which is believed everywhere, always and by all'.[4] At the same time they will also dazzle and delight with newness and freshness of life so that the Christian community is always that community which rises with Jesus to a new and still-to-be-discovered future. What we need now is the patience and the nerve to start telling the story again and let the God of mission re-create his church.

Conclusion

St Francis of Assisi famously told his followers to go into the world and preach the gospel, using words only if they had to. This injunction has often been misused to suggest that somehow words aren't important. However, it does remind us of a vital truth that actions speak louder, and that sometimes words get in the way. The instinctive catholic model of mission is incarnational and sacramental, combining worship and service. At the altar it is the actions that speak louder than the words. The same thing happens on the streets where we serve, and it is the same Christ who is worshipped and adored in sacrament and slum. The story of Christ's love is etched into the lives of his followers and into the life of his Church. We continue his mission in the Church which is itself a continuation of the incarnation, for we are baptized into his body. 'I alone must write on flesh,' says Christ in U. A. Fanthorpe's remarkable poem 'Getting It Across' (1986, p. 73).

Fresh expressions are nothing new; this is something about which we need reminding. The story – told again in changed lives, the beauty and power of sacramental worship, the dedication of service to local community – can lead to new ways of being church and to the establishment of new worshipping communities. To do anything less would be to turn the universal Church of Christ into my way of doing things.

References

Stephen Cottrell, 2006, *From the Abundance of the Heart: Catholic Evangelism for all Christians*, London: Darton Longman and Todd.
Stephen Cottrell and Tim Sledge, n.d., *Vital Statistics*, New York: Springboard Press.
Steven Croft, 2008, 'Fresh expression in a mixed economy Church: A perspective', in Steven Croft (ed.), *Mission-shaped Questions: Defining Issues for Today's Church*, London: Church House Publishing.
Steven Croft (ed.), 2008, *Mission-shaped Questions: Defining Issues for Today's Church*, London: Church House Publishing.
Vincent Donovan, 1993, *Christianity Rediscovered: An Epistle from the Masai*, London: SCM Press.
U. A. Fanthorpe, 1986, 'Getting It Across', in *Selected Poems*, London: Penguin Books.
John Hull, 2006, *Mission-Shaped Church: A Theological Response*, London: SCM Press.
Kenneth Ingram, 1936, *Basil Jellicoe*, London: The Centenary Press.
Lucy Menzies, 1947, *Father Wainright: A Record*, London: Longman, Green & Co.
W. G. Peck, 1933, *The Social Implications of the Oxford Movement*, New York City: Charles Scribner's Sons.
Alan Wilkinson, 2001, 'Jesus and the Drains', *The Franciscan*, viewed on 14 January 2009 at http://www.franciscans.org.uk/2001jan-wilkinson.html.
Rowan Williams, 2004, Address to Mission-Shaped Church Conference, 23 June.

Notes

1 I have borrowed this title from John Hull, who writes about this at greater length in his stimulating essay, 'Mission–shaped and kingdom

focused?', in Steven Croft (ed.), 2008, *Mission-shaped Questions: Defining Issues for Today's Church*, London: Church House Publishing, p. 114.

2 Proceedings of the Anglican Consultation Council: *Bonds of Affection*, 1984, ACC-6, p. 49; *Mission in a Broken World*, 1990, ACC-8, p. 101.

3 Wilkinson, 2001. In the same article he also writes: 'A Victorian slum priest, campaigning for better sanitation, was told to stop interfering in secular matters. He replied, "I speak out and fight about the drains because I believe in the Incarnation." ... This tradition of finding Jesus in the needy continued in the twentieth century. Father Basil Jellicoe, the housing pioneer, was asked why he assisted at St Martin-in-the-Fields, a church where there was no reserved sacrament. "Because the crypt is reserved for Christ's poor," he replied. A founder of SSF, Brother Douglas, believed that the gospel could be preached authentically to the poor only by those who shared their poverty.'

4 As defined by St Vincent of Lerins, written under the pseudonym Perigrinus, in AD 434.

6

Liturgically Informed Buildings

RICHARD GILES

This chapter tells the story of two communities of faith that attempt to give fresh expression to the timeless truths of the catholic tradition in a contemplative way, using re-ordered buildings as sacraments of a wider and deeper reality. But first of all, some background.

The catholic tradition in the Church of England has a mixed track record with regard to church buildings. Historically a movement that built soaring structures to speak of the mystery of God and to provide a perfect setting for the offering of splendid liturgy, it has more recently taken its eye off the ball. Secondary issues have been allowed to intervene so that, despite its high regard for the sacraments, the tradition has been neglectful of the sacramental power of buildings to shape the re-formation of liturgical practice today.

It may be that the Mass is indeed a conversion experience, but there is little evidence of this in a movement that is content with the reiteration of past glories, rather than the continual evolution of liturgical vitality. Sadly, the catholic tradition has failed to show the rest of the Church the way forward in the area of Christian life where it has most to contribute – that of renewing worship and rethinking liturgical space to help us be church today.

In the face of seemingly intractable problems over which one has little power, it is usually best to begin in that limited area where one can actually make a difference, and try to create 'something beautiful for God', as Mother Teresa used to say.

The two faith communities I have served in over the last 20

years couldn't be more different, and yet they share a common experience of renewal in which the transformation of a building was the touchstone of a regenerated community life and purpose. Our theology informed the new shape and appearance of the building's interior, and the building then helped inform and shape our liturgical practice.

St Thomas' Church in Huddersfield, West Yorkshire, was a traditional Anglo-Catholic parish in an inner-city location with a large proportion of immigrants from the Indian sub-continent and the West Indies. The 'Faith in the City' Report designated it an urban priority area, and its small but faithful congregation had for the most part come to the realization that it would be a case of 'change or die'.

Philadelphia Cathedral was also a small congregation coming to terms with a new role. Formerly a big local church in a prosperous neighbourhood, demographic changes had threatened its future until it was designated as the cathedral of the diocese of Pennsylvania in 1992. The congregation rattled around in a vast (and incredibly ugly) interior stuffed with unfilled pews, struggling to find a way forward.

Both have experienced numerical growth of 75–100 per cent since their stories began. We will look at some of the key elements in their revival.

The question of which comes first, reordered building or renewed congregation, is a classic chicken-and-egg situation. There is a circular motion of cause and effect involving the worshipper and the building set aside for worship, and it doesn't much matter where on the circle we begin. As night follows day, a lively community will impact its building, and a strong building will impact the community it houses.

In purist terms we would probably like to think that we always begin with the renewed community of faith reshaping the room in which it meets. But it is rarely as neat as that, for the influence of interior space on the way we feel and act is so immense, and the impact of any change within it so sharply felt, that spiritual renewal and architectural change tend to leapfrog over one another continually.

In both Huddersfield and Philadelphia the starting point was the appointment of a new pastor who was expected by those in authority, both locally and in the diocese, to bring change. Change, as part and parcel of the gospel, was a message that was posted up on every available surface – preaching, teaching, written material, etc. – from day one, and was repeated continuously.

From that single theological and strategic starting point physical changes were sought which would spell out the theory in readily understood practice. Both buildings posed severe challenges to renewal of any kind. St Thomas' in Huddersfield was a noble edifice designed by George Gilbert Scott in 1859, but its interior layout, with fixed pews on slightly raised platforms throughout the nave, restricted the congregation to a very traditional understanding of the congregation's role in worship. A notice in the sacristy that read 'The Peace is not shared in this church', indicates the way in which liturgy as previously experienced there further reinforced such restrictions. On my first Sunday in Huddersfield the Peace was shared, no matter how uncomfortable for all concerned, because reconciliation should be central to Christian liturgy. Likewise, from then on coffee was served afterwards on every Sunday, not just on some, because hospitality is intrinsic to Christian liturgy.

Following very soon upon the heels of these liturgical changes, explained as part of a theological rationale, came changes to the physical structure which would further the process of renewal. The diocesan bishop (at that time David Hope) came up with a bit of cash from his discretionary fund with which we refurbished the sacristy, creating a small chapel for daily worship (relegating clergy and servers to a closet behind the organ). These developments set out, for all to see and experience, the direction things were heading. Seating was around the perimeter on benches cannibalized from old pews, and a new altar table was made at the local high school and set in the midst. The design aimed at elegant simplicity and was a no-go area for the lace, banners and statues that proliferated elsewhere in the building.

The effect of this starter project cannot be overestimated in terms of our Christian formation. Here was a truly 'liturgically informed space' helping us to understand who we were. Weekday congregations were no longer an audience scattered the length of the north aisle, peering at a distant altar, but a community conscious of one another and interacting with one another in the offering of the liturgy. Countless talks and explanations may have done the trick eventually, but Bishop David's financial assistance was our short cut to revelation.

The building in Philadelphia was equally restrictive, and this was compounded by an extremely gloomy and ugly interior. However, on my second Sunday there we began a liturgy of journey, whereby we sat in chairs at the west end for the ministry of the Word, and moved (through acres of empty pews) to the east end for the ministry of the Sacrament.

This initial launch into an experience of journey, which has continued ever since, was solidified with better furniture, such as a square altar and a lectern (both discovered unused at Church House), and a movable font, which was set up at the west end near the entrance. Additionally, the bishop's chair was brought out from the corner of the chancel to face west and preside over the liturgical space. Thus were the main elements of the cathedral's ministry set out, albeit in provisional and less-than-satisfactory form.

At this point theology leap-frogged over architecture again, as we entered a period of teaching and reflection, a process aided by these preliminary practical changes all around us. At Huddersfield the annual parish weekend-away became the highlight of our calendar, and was the occasion when (often with an outside envisioner) we were lifted to fresh vision in a relaxed, unhurried atmosphere, liberated from the chores of home and from the ever-present weight of the building we had known and loved. At Philadelphia we never got into the parish weekend-away routine, but Americans tend to be ready to talk about any issue at the drop of a hat, and we somehow got through the same agenda of study and reflection at home.

At that point physical change once again leap-frogged ahead, helping us consolidate our thinking. In both Huddersfield and Philadelphia the crucial period of transformation for the community did not start the day we walked into the newly refurbished building, but the day we walked *out* of it, into the exile of temporary accommodation. The experience of moving from a restrictive worship space into a neutral space (a church hall in one case, and office meeting rooms in another), proved life-changing.

Like mechanics learning about engines, we took our life of worship apart, spread all the components on the floor, found out how they worked, and reassembled everything into a new form that hummed with life. We were free to sit in various configurations, move from one room to another, learn how to make music without an organ, get used to sitting close to one another, to having fun, and to discard that which we found we could live without. At Huddersfield, for example, as a parish accustomed to kneeling for communion, we had no choice but to receive standing. Nothing was said about kneeling ever again. Caught up in a new adventure, we collectively forgot old habits and adopted new ones (which were in fact found to be far more authentic in terms of primitive Christian practice anyway).

These provisional 'tents' of our period in exile, though inadequate and unsatisfactory in many ways, proved to be extremely effective in shaping our liturgical life. Once again a process of learning which otherwise may have taken years was telescoped into a matter of months.

A vital part of learning how to worship during our exiles was making music. This sprang from the theological conviction that (as in a monastic community) the whole assembly is the choir, and that we are called to make music together, not listen to others do so on our behalf. Suddenly we were no longer a congregation rattling around in a vast barn of a building with an organ thundering around us, but a group of friends in a room learning some new songs, gathered round a grand piano along with any other instruments we could muster. Escaping from the confines of particular hymnbooks with their preponderance of Victorian hymns, we emerged, blinking, into the daylight of songs written by Christians today from across the world, with melodies we found ourselves humming throughout the week. We learnt responsorial singing, rounds, chants for cantor and people, songs from other traditions, as well as chants from the ancient Church.

This period of exile, which lasted between 12 and 18 months, was in both cases unavoidable because of the construction work going on in the main church building. However, it was so effective in liturgical formation that, if one didn't have a reason for a little exile, I would suggest dreaming one up for the sake of the kingdom.

At the end of our period of camping-out it was time for the great day when we entered into our inheritance; a church building redesigned and refurnished in accordance with the principles and practice we had worked on together up to that point. It was to be a building tailor-made for our needs, instead of one that imposed its agenda on us.

In both cases the new interiors were stripped of their old furniture. A level floor, with a single unifying material (French limestone in Philadelphia, soft green carpet in Huddersfield), was established throughout the nave, and in both cases chairs replaced pews. Both interiors gained spaciousness and freedom from clutter and visual busyness.

At Huddersfield the central feature was an altar constructed with stones reused from the old church and from a neighbouring industrial facility. This honoured the catholic roots of the parish's life, and stood as an immovable symbol of all that was central to its thinking. A new font, by the same local sculptor who made the altar, was placed at the entrance to the worship space, with water continually flowing from a higher to a lower level.

At Philadelphia the baptismal font (in the spacious south aisle) and the bishop's cathedra were the only fixed immovable objects – being built of matching stone, with the wooden altar table and ambo being movable (though as infrequently as possible). The stone bench of the presbyterium (the synthronos), on either side of the bishop's chair, is continued right around

Huddersfield interior before

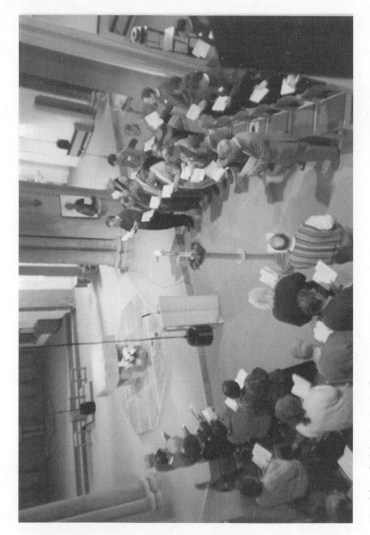

Huddersfield interior after

Philadelphia interior before

Philadelphia interior after

the perimeter of the nave in order to symbolize that we in the diocese were a community of faith gathered round the waters of baptism under the presidency of our bishop.

We were able to recreate the configuration of an early Christian basilica. Due to the space being larger than at Huddersfield, the four liturgical foci of chair, font, ambo and altar table stood out in greater prominence against a backdrop of stark simplicity. Many visitors likened it to a Cistercian monastic interior, which encouraged us.[1]

Both interiors are liturgically informed buildings because their appearance (as in churches in every previous period of Christian history) reflects the theological convictions and liturgical practices of the communities who use them. They are superb tools for teaching us who we are, and what we are about. Each time we assemble in them for the Eucharist we are helped by their physical form, so redolent of early Christian practice, to remember our calling and our purpose.

What might we discern from these two stories as salient features of a rediscovery of worship in the catholic and contemplative tradition?

Learning to be church

Many worshippers return home from a parish weekend-away, or an inspiring training event, raring to go, but find their hopes shipwrecked on the hidden rocks of vested interest and territorialism in the land of status quo. Many parishes are really fiefdoms that, over time, corner the market for particular tasks. At both Huddersfield and Philadelphia this was addressed by changing the whole way the assembly operated, beginning with the offering of the Sunday liturgy as a corporate exercise.

The congregation was divided up into a number of teams of approximately 12 members each. A team was on duty each Sunday to make sure the liturgy happened. Leaders were chosen, and membership put together, by clergy and lay leaders who ensured that each team had 'experts' in each field. Except for worship leading, the team members on duty fulfilled all the essential roles of sacristans, welcomers, readers, intercessors, thurifers, servers, those presenting the gifts at the altar, coffee makers and clearer-uppers.

The teams were formed for the purpose of fulfilling liturgical tasks but, if geographically feasible, had the potential to grow into house groups where team members could deepen their faith and fellowship. Team leaders became the eyes and ears of the pastor, and co-workers in pastoral care, attending a monthly meeting with the clergy.

Theological exploration, undertaken together, was a significant feature of our common life, and teams provided a safe place where people could discuss, ask questions, express doubts, and find they were not alone. The Christian faith was for us more about asking the honest questions than knowing the right answers.

In weekly and monthly meetings of various kinds, often over a meal, there developed a culture of mutual trust in which questions could be asked and insights pursued. Mindful of all those who seek God but who cannot abide what the Church has done in the name of Christ over the last 2,000 years, we sought to remove some of the obstacles to faith, the misunderstandings that needlessly deter others, and to pursue truth wherever it led.[2]

Learning to worship

Learning to worship again, at both Huddersfield and Philadelphia, unlocked the energy of the Spirit among us. We became who we were meant to be. Key elements in rediscovering the liturgy were:

1 **Preparation.** People often forget why they come to church, and often there is a continual hubbub of noise up to the moment that the liturgy begins. After the liturgy is the time to socialize. Before the liturgy we would greet one another briefly on arrival, and then take our places in the assembly to prepare in silence to meet the living God.

In both places we worked to establish the norm of silence before worship, raising dramatically the level of anticipation. In Philadelphia this was given added force by the use of the morning office as a preparation for the Mass. Thirty minutes before the main liturgy we would sing a simple version of Morning Prayer – office hymn, psalm, reading, canticle and prayers – to provide, as it were, a 'raft' of contemplative prayer on which the Mass would float.

2 **Journey.** All too often liturgy becomes a static experience, whereas the whole Judeo-Christian story is grounded in the experience of journey, travelling light as spiritual nomads seeking the city that is to come. In Huddersfield, the whole assembly would move, at the offertory, from the nave to the chancel in order to stand around the altar where we would offer the eucharistic prayer and share communion together. After this the people would return to their seats for a time of reflection. In Philadelphia the experience of journey was even more pronounced by the large space through which the whole assembly moved in a three-part journey. Gathering first around the baptismal pool to make their peace with God and one another, the assembly then moved on to sit around the ambo to be formed by the Scriptures; after this they moved again to stand around the altar for the Eucharistic prayer (those who needed seats were of course given them).

3 **Silence.** Although the catholic tradition can teach us much about contemplative prayer, it seems not to practice what it preaches when it comes to liturgy. Our liturgies tend to be as stuffed with words as our liturgical spaces are with bric-a-brac. In both Huddersfield and Philadelphia, periods of silence were maintained after the readings and after communion, being announced at beginning and end by the striking of a gong (the type easily obtainable from Buddhist web sites) so that the assembly could relax into them.

4 **Shared priesthood.** The downside of the traditional catholic focus on the sacred (ordained) priesthood has been a narrowing of the concept of sacred vocation and an impoverishment

of the call to priesthood shared by the whole eucharistic assembly.[3]

There are several ways in which the insight of the priestly community can be made real and tangible:

- **Seating.** If the assembly is lined up in rigid rows facing the front they will continue to feel like an audience watching a show. Seating that encircles a central focus, whether of word or sacrament, immediately suggests engagement in a shared enterprise. A community of participating ministers begins slowly to emerge from the collection of observers.

- **Ritual.** On one Sunday at Huddersfield, about 5 minutes before the Mass was to begin (which is sometimes when the best ideas come!), the director of music and I conceived the idea of inviting the whole assembly to join in the entrance procession, and in pairs to approach the altar table and to reverence it with a kiss. Traditionally the president alone does this, but here was an opportunity for all present to realize their own share in the priestly task. It was a deeply moving and unforgettable moment.

  A further development at Philadelphia was the custom of the president vesting each person who addressed the assembly – reader, intercessor, preacher, cantor, etc. – with the president's stole, making visible the authority and trust vested in that person, at that moment, by the whole assembly.

- **Posture.** At Philadelphia the whole assembly was asked, when standing around the altar table for the eucharistic prayer, to adopt the *orans* posture, where hands are raised in supplication to God. As with reverencing the altar, this posture was formerly adopted by the ordained priest alone. Now it became the shared posture of the whole priestly assembly.

- **Communion.** At both places the method of sharing communion also heightened the sense of shared priestly access to holy things. After receiving the holy bread where they stood encircling the altar table, each member of the assembly was invited to approach the altar table and take the cup into their own hands.

5 **Presidency.** All this requires a pastor who can preside over the Eucharist in a special way, sure of his/her own authority, but happy to let go. The sensitive president is one who delights in drawing forth from the whole assembly, and then co-ordinating the gifts and ministries contained within it. Like a gifted choreographer, she wills to see the dance brought to life.[4]

The president should preside in such a way that, without intrusion, everything is carefully co-ordinated without anyone being consciously aware (to read more about presiding see my *Creating Uncommon Worship*, Canterbury Press (2004), Part 2, section 4).

6 **Reverence and awe.** Much nonsense is spouted about 'losing transcendence' when we reorder church buildings. Nothing could be further from the truth, provided we take great care to do everything well. The solemn dignity of the Eucharist, celebrated with a sense of wonder and delight in a space of stunning beauty and utter simplicity, is a deeply spiritual experience. Only the very best of everything will do: 'Because the assembly gathers in the presence of God to celebrate his saving deeds, the liturgy's climate is one of awe, mystery, wonder, reverence, thanksgiving and praise. So it cannot be satisfied with anything less than the beautiful.'[5]

7 **Appropriate music,** the most essential element of a renewed liturgy, played a vital part in both Huddersfield and Philadelphia. It is quite astonishing that in the third millennium we continue to sing hymns framed in Victorian language and theology. The wealth of new material of the highest standard – by the likes of Bernadette Farrell, John Bell, Paul Inwood and Christopher Walker – is enormous, and to neglect such richness is inexcusable.

Vital steps in the renewal of music were:
- A group of singers and musicians that replaced the robed choir.
- Singers and musicians rejoining the rest of the community, seated among them.
- A variety of instruments augmenting the organ.
- Music culled from a wide variety of sources.

- The whole assembly understood as the choir, with frequent practice together.
8 **Hospitality**. To offer refreshments after the liturgy was essential in both places as a means of greeting and befriending the newcomer, and consolidating community life. It was seen as an extension of the liturgy, almost part of it, for Christian worship without hospitality is deficient, theologically as well as nutritionally.

Learning to make liturgical space

All the above key elements have architectural or design consequences. We cannot mean business about renewing worship if we have no intention of renewing the room in which worship is offered. Certain physical alterations will be necessary to enable us to do what we say we wish to do. An appropriate architectural setting also helps form us and keep us in good habits.

1 **Prayerful preparation** will require two distinct spaces in which to carry out the mutually conflicting activities of welcome and prayer. In other words a narthex or entrance area will need to be constructed, usually within the envelope of the existing building.
2 **A liturgy of participation** will require a seating plan expressive of the community's nature. Fixed pews facing in a single direction are an immense obstacle to such self-understanding, and usually have to go. They should be replaced by chairs (or perhaps short, light-weight benches) configured in a way that is suggestive of communal life and of shared endeavour.
3 **A liturgy of movement** will require a fair amount of unrestricted space in which the assembly can move together.
4 **A community that prays** and appreciates silence needs a church building with lots of empty space, as well as corners in which to curl up; it needs to be both spacious and intimate. Out with junk and clutter, in with serene open space and just a few foci of prayer, where candles can be lit and silent prayer entered into.

5 **A liturgy focused afresh** on initiation, word and sacrament, will need just a single focus for each of the key elements of worship: a font in a prominent and spacious location, with accessible water; a single ambo in the midst of the people, where the word is read and preached; an altar table, also in the midst, around which the whole assembly can stand to offer the eucharistic prayer.

6 **A community that prides itself on welcome** must have the facilities to enflesh the theory. A hall across a churchyard, or even down a corridor, might as well be on the other side of the moon. The opportunity to join the regulars in a cup of coffee must be immediate, and seamlessly joined to the end of the liturgy. Architecturally, this will demand a space at the back of the church, where hospitality can be offered. If a proper narthex is some way off, just clear a space, wheel in a trolley and plug in an urn.

(For a more detailed treatment of these design issues see my *Re-pitching the Tent*, 2004, London: Canterbury Press.)

In the two stories related above we see how liturgically informed buildings have arisen from the aspirations of the faith community, but have then helped shape and mould the ongoing life and quest of that community. Theology and architecture, theory and practice, are in continual interaction – people and building informing and shaping one another as the journey continues.

When these two aspects of our common life stop 'talking' to each other buildings become untouchable shrines, and the people who use them either prisoners or curators. Then we are doomed. So then, long may the dialogue continue as it has done down the ages. May we work on our buildings, and may they work on us, until we arrive at that 'city that has foundations, whose architect and builder is God' (Heb. 11.10).

Notes

1 For images of the reordered space see www.philadelphiacathedral. org.

2 The life of John Robinson exemplified the relentless search for the truth with no reservations of any kind, and without fear as to the outcome (see Eric James, 1989, *A Life of Bishop A. T. Robinson*, London: Fount Publishing).

3 This is not the same thing as the 'priesthood of all believers' – a kind of protestant nightmare in which each believer is his or her own priest – but the priesthood shared by the whole community which constitutes the body of Christ. It is the priestly call to God's people contained in 1 Peter 2.9, 'But you are a chosen race, a royal priesthood, a holy nation', is clearly a collective, not an individual call.

4 In a delightful tribute to John Betjeman, it was said: 'He is their Diaghilev for the evening, enchanting them all just as he enchants crabbed clergymen and pernickety architectural historians, making them feel that theirs is the only universe that counts, and that they are kings of it' (Ferdinand Mount, 2008, *Cold Cream: My Early Life and Other Mistakes*, London: Bloomsbury Publishing, p. 66).

5 National Conference of US Catholic Bishops, 1986, 'Environment and Art in Catholic Worship'. A PDF of the document can be downloaded from www.dow.org/documents/EACWstudyDOC.doc.

7

Liturgical Issues and Fresh Expressions

CARL TURNER

They say that time changes things, but you actually have to change them yourself.
(Warhol, 1975, p. 111)

To be truly authentic the local church must make real connections with the community in which it has been formed. Such connections are hallmarks of authenticity that are recognized by those who live locally. However, for a community's liturgical life to be authentic and true to the apostolic tradition it must also look beyond itself and relate to the wider Church. Such are the tensions faced by parish communities every week, but especially by fresh expressions of church within the catholic tradition of the Church of England. How rooted should the liturgical life of a fresh expression community be in the life of the wider Church? How crucial is their relationship with the bishop in forming the hallmarks of the catholic Church? It may be helpful to ponder what the essential characteristics of Anglican liturgical worship are. For example, how creative or explorative can a fresh expression be? Are there elements of the liturgical life of the Church that are significantly connected with a sense of Anglican identity? What relationship does the liturgical life of the Church have with differing local cultures? What is given and what can be changed or reinvented? And how can we tell the difference between what is truly a fresh expression and what is simply a tinkering with established practice to make it more appealing to those who find traditional church dull?

One of the glories of the catholic revival of the Church of England was the rediscovery of that which was ancient and long established and yet largely no longer part of its liturgical memory. The development of the ritualistic movement in the late nineteenth century coincided with the industrial revolution and a huge change in the social fabric of England. In many respects it could be argued that those early ritualists were attempting to find a fresh expression of being the catholic Church in this country. The affect of the ritualistic movement and the accompanying ritualistic trials was phenomenal; such was the passion generated that even members of the Church of England were incited to riot! The expansion of ceremonial and catholic practices was, in some ways, in stark contrast to the more sedate and cerebral exploration of the life of the patristic church by the original Tractarians. The ritualistic movement made a significant connection with real peoples' lives. By the end of Queen Victoria's reign, the great majority of people lived in cities, and the movement touched the lives of many poor, sick and marginalized, offering them a glimpse of heaven that such people had not seen for centuries. It is interesting to ponder if the Anglo-Catholic movement would have had such a profound influence on our nation had it not have coincided with the huge demographic and cultural changes that happened in the latter half of the nineteenth century.

What the Anglo-Catholic movement discovered was that the worship of God needed to touch all the senses and become a transforming power in people's lives. At the same time it was linked with social action and pastoral care, and with a zeal that had not been experienced since the previous century with the great Evangelical revival, and leaders such as John and Charles Wesley. It is interesting to note that whenever great leaders of the Church have pushed the boundaries of both worship and social action, they have met great opposition. Can the same be said of those leading fresh expressions today?

I was a priest for 11 years in an East London parish that was the product of the Anglo-Catholic revival. Within the parish was the first Franciscan Friary since the Reformation, established in 1894 by Fr Andrew and the Society of the Divine Compassion. The history of the society, which later became part of the Society of St Francis, is characterized by the offering of the best to God in worship and a commitment to the poor. Fr Andrew's diary entry on 11 December 1894 read, 'It makes one feel very sad to hear the children praying, "Give us this dy our dyly [sic] bread", when one knows there is nothing at home for them.' And on 18 December 1894, he wrote, 'The poverty here is something fearful. I have found families without even the light of a candle sitting silently and starving in the dark' (Burne, 1948, p. 32).

One hundred years later, I experienced the very same conditions in some of the most deprived parts of that London borough. By then, however, much of the Church's work had been replaced by that of the statutory agencies. Whereas at the turn of the twentieth century the parish had run a school, had a number of religious sisters serving as midwives and a group of priests and brothers working tirelessly for the relief of poverty and disease – sometimes at great cost to themselves, by the late twentieth century the liturgical life of the Church and the social action of the parish had been separated. Consequently a number of once large, vibrant and well-staffed Anglo-Catholic churches were now small, fragile and worried communities trying to justify their existence. I mention this because I think loving social action was an important reason for the success of the Anglo-Catholic revival. I also think it is something that catholic and contemplative fresh expressions would do well to ponder. No amount of creative liturgy can fill the gap in people's lives caused by worry, poverty, disease, redundancy, debt or addiction; worship can only be truly transforming if it affects a change in our lives.

In Luke's Gospel, a lawyer asked Jesus which was the greatest commandment. Jesus turned the question back on the lawyer:

Jesus said to him, 'What is written in the law? What do you read there?' He answered, 'You shall love the Lord your

God with all your heart, and with all your soul, and with all your strength, and with all your mind; and your neighbour as yourself.' And he said to him, 'You have given the right answer; do this, and you will live.'
(Luke 10.25–28)

Prompting the lawyer to put his faith and knowledge into action in turn led to Jesus to tell one of most well known of parables – the Good Samaritan. The essential link between love of God and love of neighbour must be explicit if worship is to be transforming. Worship that connects with the lives of real people will inevitably blur the boundaries between the sacred and the secular; between the tradition of the Church and the cultural context of the community; between heaven and earth. The greatest test of any catholic fresh expression will be the transformative nature of its worship, whose authenticity is marked as much by the making of connections as by loyalty to any inheritance of faith and order.

> The drama of church history, as well as the adventure of our own discipleship, is that there is always the possibility of transformation and renewal, and the agent of transformation is always and only Jesus Christ. Renewal in the Church has only occurred when individuals have turned to Jesus and told him, 'They have no wine', and been prepared to be the instruments of his transforming power. When that happens, though his glory is manifested only to the few, the Church is rescued from its failure and the wedding feast continues.
> (Holloway, 1992, p. 15)

Desirable though it may seem to some, the Church of England does not have any kind of liturgical police force; it is therefore unlikely that any bishop could enforce uniformity of liturgical practice across his diocese. Most know that this is a very good thing. The second half of the twentieth century saw the development of new kinds of theological exploration, influenced by greater insights in the worlds of medical research, sociological, psychological and political study. The development of specific brands of theology grew out of the desire people had for theology that would connect with the heart of their life-style or culture – rather than conforming to what were essentially white, Western ways of thinking. The 'Faith in the City Report' raised more than a few establishment eyebrows in 1985, but the development of Feminist, Black and Queer theological frameworks, alongside a parallel socio-political agenda, meant that it was only a matter of time before the Church would find itself challenged in its liturgical forms and language. For, as long as liturgy is to be the work of the people, the life-style and culture of the particular context in which a community springs up will influence its liturgical expression.

This has caused no small amount of pain to the Anglican Communion. In 2003 when the Bishop of New Westminster, Canada, authorized rites for the blessing of same-sex unions, many members of the Communion were deeply anxious. In Britain, the established Church now finds itself part of a society that blesses life-long same-sex partnerships in law. Civil partnerships, like marriages contracted at a register office, are to be devoid of religious ceremony, sentiment and even religious music. However, many gay and lesbian couples are committed members of churches and play an important part in their daily life. How can their own language, life-style and worldview be reflected in the liturgical life of the community when, for some, this life-style is at odds with the Christian journey per se? Given that Black and Feminist Theology has only been able to influence liturgy in a minimal way, it is to be expected that Queer Theology will have an even more difficult relationship with the established Church. All this points to the emergence of small, fragile and yet vibrant communities, where risk-taking and exploration is essential to the pilgrimage of faith. In this respect, fresh expressions are simply one phenomenon of an increasing tension between the call to orthodoxy and conformity on one hand, and for freedom of expression and liberty in the Spirit on the other.

In 1982, the Archbishop of Milwaukee, Rembert Weakland

OSB – who was appointed five years previously by Pope Paul VI in the heady days after Vatican II – suggested that the washing of feet at the Maundy Thursday Mass of the Lord's Supper was no longer a culturally potent symbol for North Americans. That same year, St John's Basilica used bowls of water at the liturgy and the assembly was invited to come forward and wash their hands, rather than their feet. This was a direct departure from the liturgical tradition of the Church in several different ways: first, from the story of the last supper as told in John's Gospel; secondly, from the collective liturgical memory of the Roman Catholic Church worldwide; and thirdly, from the normative account found 'in the book'. The Archbishop's suggestion also raised two important questions: first, how do we respond to the story of Jesus Christ so that it connects with real self? And second, what is essential, and what is not, in telling the story of faith?

Archbishop Weakland brought the experience of everyday Milwaukee folk to the heart of the liturgy of the Lord's Supper. This is a story of inculturation, not at the periphery of the liturgy, but at its very heart. Inculturation is a two-way process in which both the Church and the external culture are affected and, in certain ways, both are subtly changed. It is a process that has had a huge impact on the Catholic Church in the past and is still very much shaping its future. In the encyclical 'On the permanent validity of the Church's missionary mandate', promulgated on 7 December 1990, Pope John Paul taught that inculturation was not only a tool by which the authenticity of the gospel might be proclaimed, but also an essential way in which the mission of the Church might be deepened:

> Through inculturation the Church makes the Gospel incarnate in different cultures and at the same time introduces peoples, together with their cultures, into her own community. She transmits to them her own values, at the same time taking the good elements that already exist in them and renewing them from within. Through inculturation the Church,

for her part, becomes a more intelligible sign of what she is, and a more effective instrument of mission.
(Pope John Paul II, 1990, pp. 85–7)

However, the process of inculturation may be one-sided when the exercise of power by one cultural form results in the loss of power by the other. The Church can think that it is being changed through contact with other contexts and cultures when in reality it is doing little to challenge or change its core beliefs or teachings, and is simply picking and choosing that which fits the already established pattern of ideas. Some call this *acculturation*, where the interaction of two cultures does not necessarily result in significant change in either, both remaining distinct and intact. In liturgical terms, acculturation is suggested when the liturgical form is not changed by the social context in which it is expressed; for example:

> Sometimes the liturgy borrows cultural elements without interiorly assimilating them, that is, without allowing them to become part and parcel of its language and ritual expression ... A classic example is the way the liturgy was acculturated during the time of the baroque. Unable to penetrate the canonical and rubrical barriers that securely guarded the Tridentine liturgy, the culture of the baroque remained in the periphery of the liturgy. The baroque manifestations of festivity and exuberance were not absorbed by the texts and rites of the Mass; there was merely an external juxtaposition of liturgical rite and cultural forms.
> (Chupungco, 1989, p. 27)

Fresh expressions are inherently different, which may, in part, be to do with the exercise of power within them. Traditional church planting often involves a larger parent-church sending out some of it members to produce another form of itself, rather like a gardener using cuttings from a parent-plant to propagate others. The propagation of cuttings results in an exact replica of the parent plant; this process can be so successful that the parent-plant might actually be stripped of all its shoots and die in the production of numerous copies. This gardening analogy has been applicable to the Church for many years. An ironic example of this is the former Methodist Church building in St Barnabas Road, Leicester. At its height it sent out many missionaries overseas and, particularly, into India. It has since ceased to be a Christian church building and is now the Shree Hindu Temple and Community Centre, being run by the very same people the missionaries had been sent to.

Marty Haugen tells of a story recounted to him about the dangers of making assumptions about inculturation:

Pia Moriarty, an anthropologist, related a story to me about the Hmong people who come from the highlands between Laos and Cambodia. When missionaries first made contact with the Hmong, the Hmong told the missionaries rich stories of their history and vision. Because they had no written language, the missionaries said, 'We can help you develop a written language so that you can put these stories down into books.' The Hmong replied, 'We used to have books, but one day the books fell into the rice and we ate them.' The missionaries, not quite understanding, said, 'It's too bad that you ate your books.' 'No,' the Hmong told them, 'now we have eaten the words, so we can tell the stories to you.' (Haugen, 1998)

Learning the language of those around is crucial if their stories are to be bound up with our own. We sometimes forget that the Book of the Gospels, carried in procession, once started with small, fragile Jewish communities who were very used to sharing the stories of faith and of the shared tradition orally. This tradition remained in the Church for some time and is, therefore, an authentic way for the Church to keep fresh the story of redemption. Liturgically, the sense of an oral tradition is also important. For example, the practice of the early Church was that the eucharistic president would be skilled in extemporary prayer. We are given a clear example of this in the writings of Justin Martyr, from the mid second century: 'He who presides raises prayers and Eucharists to heaven as much as he can' (*Apologia*, 1:67). Hippolytus, writing at the beginning of the third century, makes this skill even more explicit:

> The bishop shall give thanks according to all that was said above. It is not at all necessary that he prays with the very same words given above, as though by an effort of memory giving thanks to God. Each shall pray whatever is according to his ability. If someone has the ability to pray a lengthy and solemn prayer, that is well. If someone else, in praying, offers a short prayer, this is not to be prevented. That prayer must only be correct in orthodoxy.
> (*Apostolic Tradition*, 9:3–5)

The president in the Eucharist prayer could express this skill by using little or no set text and allowing cultural themes, local language or dialect, and the needs of the local community, to colour the prayer; but the canons of the Church of England do not permit this. There is however, a rule in *New Patterns for Worship* that allows for special prefaces to be written and prayed. So what are the givens and how much flexibility is there for catholic fresh expressions? Bearing in mind all that has been said above, this exploration can be tabulated as in Table 1.

Looking at the table we begin to see that the relationship between traditional worship and fresh expressions of worship is quite fluid; some manifestations are, arguably, a departing not only from that which is authorized, but also from the story of our faith. Others are merely slight variations of the received tradition. To take an extreme example, one could easily argue that using anything other than bread and wine at the Eucharist is to depart entirely from that which Jesus ordained; after all, can one truly celebrate the Eucharist without bread and wine? But the use of other elements in the act of communion can be very powerful. Clearly, for many in the Church there are certain givens, to depart from which is to depart from the

Table 1

	Current rules of the Church of England	Various 'expressions' of this			
President	Must be an ordained priest, or bishop (if present).	Concelebration.	Lay presidency.	Lay co-celebration with a priest.	Lay concelebration.
Elements	Must be bread and wine fermented of the grape.	Could be coffee and cake, or some other combination of food.	There may be no elements at all.		
Texts	Must be an authorized eucharistic prayer.	The whole prayer is extemporary.	Parts of the prayer are extemporary.	Prayers are written according to need.	No texts or words are used, only symbolic action.

Church's core understanding of the eucharistic celebration. Taking a less extreme example, there are churches that do not use alcoholic wine, which is, strictly speaking, contrary to the teaching of the Church of England. Some will argue that at least it looks like wine (it may even be made from grapes). So how far can one go? Perhaps it is worth considering whether there are different orders of priority. Table 2 differentiates, for catholic fresh expression communities, between what could be called primary and secondary concepts, or, perhaps, essential and not-so-essential elements.

Table 2

Primary concept (essential)	Secondary concept (not so essential)
Ordained priest or bishop.	All other ministries.
Bread and wine.	All other symbols, ceremonial and symbolic actions.
The structure of the rite.	The actual texts used.

Referring back to the writings of Hippolytus, the president was one acknowledged to have skill in the offering of extemporary prayer – the Great Thanksgiving – but, and importantly, Hippolytus tells us that there is not absolute flexibility, that there are various elements of the thanksgiving which must be used, 'That prayer must only be correct in orthodoxy' (*Apostolic Tradition* 9:3–5). Is Hippolytus referring here to what we have described as the primary, essential, elements of liturgical prayer?

We can approach this dilemma from a different angle, by prioritizing the importance of texts and ministries in terms of appropriateness for the community in question, by having a high regard for the context or culture in which the assembly meets. Table 3 illustrates that this is a decidedly different way of looking at the liturgy.

Table 3

Primary (essential)	Secondary (not so essential)
Ministry to the community.	Authorized ministers and priests.
Sense of communion.	Bread and wine, coffee and cake, fish and chips.
Connection with local culture.	Prayer books, authorized texts, local texts.

Many in the catholic movement will question both the ecclesiological authenticity of such a community, and the appropriateness of a liturgy that places more emphasis on the local context and less on the shared, received tradition of the Church. 'Messy Church' is a good example of a fresh expression community that finds itself in a middle ground where the boundaries between liturgy and social life are somewhat blurred. Its liturgy is quite formal, although the texts used are written locally, bread and wine is used and a priest presides. It gives us an insight into how an Anglo-Catholic community might gently push the boundaries whilst retaining the elements vital to its understanding of what it is to be the visible Church. It is an example of a community that has made connections with the local culture, that takes the risk of sharing the Good News in ways that challenge those within and outside the Church, and yet retains that which is primary to the liturgical expression of the Church in that place.

There are many examples of principally lay-led communities whose focus is entirely outward looking in terms of Christian service, who yet retain a catholic spirituality of great depth and wide resonance. The community of Sant'Egidio, which is based in what was originally a very poor neighbourhood, Trastevere, Rome, is one such example; prayer, communicating the gospel, friendship with the poor and a commitment to peace have been at the heart of this Roman Catholic fresh expression for the past 40 years. At their daily prayer gathering in Santa Maria,

Trastevere, one or two priests may be seen loitering at the back but the service, including the sermon, is entirely lay-led. Food is served in the church regularly and, after the principal Mass on Christmas Day, the church becomes a dining room for the poor and the homeless. The linking of prayer with service to the poor is, of course, at the heart of many religious communities and it finds its heartbeat, within the Christian tradition, in the exchange between Jesus and the lawyer.

Clearly, for the Sant'Egidio community there is a recognizable liturgical framework within which the prayer of the community is voiced. It is perhaps harder to hear the authentic voice of a fresh expression for which community formation or service to the poor, and not worship, is the reason for its existence. Many Anglo-Catholics would question whether a community that doesn't worship could be described as a fresh expression of church at all. Similarly, how does one avoid creating a church whose worship is gimmicky, trying out a few (and often not so fresh) ideas to spice up an otherwise dull liturgy? Those who are prepared to take risks by exploring some of what has been described above can truly claim the term 'fresh expression'. Some ambient music, a plethora of video screens, lots of candles and dry ice do not, on their own, make a church a 'fresh expression', any more than filling a building with shrines and incense makes those within it Anglo-Catholic. If, however, those responsible for creating the liturgy are prepared to wrestle with the hard questions lying at the heart of the community, then the journey of discovery has begun. It is a journey in the course of which, many people will play a part. It is not about the way the liturgy is celebrated but how the liturgy becomes a vehicle for conversion:

What is needed is not more liturgical piety. On the contrary, one of the greatest enemies of the Liturgy is liturgical piety. The Liturgy is not to be treated as an aesthetic experience or a therapeutic exercise. Its unique function is to reveal to us the Kingdom of God. This is what we commemorate eternally. The remembrance, the *anamnesis* of the Kingdom is

the source of everything else in the Church. It is this that theology strives to bring to the world. And it comes even to a 'post-Christian' world as the gift of healing, of redemption and of joy.
(Schmemann, 1990, p. 100)

The French Roman Catholic Joseph Gelineau, who died in 2008, was a formative figure for many whose vocations were fostered in the Church during the 1970s and 80s, my own included. Gelineau is principally remembered for his musicianship and in connection with the liturgical renewal of the Roman Catholic Church following Vatican II. However, as a Jesuit he was, and remained until the end of his life, a pastor and teacher; all his work and explorations were marked by the discernment of the truth of the gospel that lies at the heart of the Church's liturgy. For him, the words and symbolic actions of the liturgy were not enough in themselves; they had to be authentic so that, to use his own favoured expression, they revealed the transparency of the gospel (1978, pp. 114 ff.). The making of connections between the liturgy and the real world is crucial if the liturgical life of the Church is to remain authentic. Authenticity is not just about being faithful to the inherited tradition; it is also about interpreting that tradition in the light of new social contexts. Catholic fresh expressions will always feel the tension between the need to be faithful to the centrality of Christian worship, and the necessity of encouraging the growth of communities that are able to make new and essential connections with the local context. These connections may take the leadership of such fresh expressions into uncharted waters; in order to make fresh and vibrant connections with those around them, they may find that that which is at the very heart of their daily lives is challenged. This is where Gelineau is truly helpful by insisting that the authenticity of liturgies is such that they reveal the transparency of the gospel. If a fresh expression is to become anything more than a slightly more interesting version of the original, then leaders, and especially the clergy, will have to learn to hold lightly to those things they thought (or even taught or preached) were essential for catholic identity. Gelineau puts this very plainly: 'Solemnities are vain, words are empty, music a waste of time, prayer useless and rites nothing but lies if they are not transfigured by justice and mercy' (1978, p. 122). The development of catholic fresh expressions may be a thorn in the side of the Church to many, but it is also the chance for the catholicity of the Church to be more authentic, God-centred, inclusive and, ultimately, real.

I remember, as a young curate, hearing many talks by those responsible for stewardship in the diocese. There was a favoured way of describing the typical church, and where most of its active members (and money) came from. A diagram of a church building would be shown with a small group of people around the altar in the sanctuary, a larger number in the Nave of the church and even more in the porch! We were told that 20 per cent of the church members (those in the sanctuary) gave 80 per cent of the finances of the community, whilst 80 per cent of the church members gave only 20 per cent between them. Those in the porch – the largest group – had yet to give anything at all. The object, we were told, was simple – we had to move people from the street to the altar. Catholic fresh expressions know of the tension between finding Jesus in the people who never even get as far as the porch, and the significance of being gathered around the altar; importantly however, this form of worship is not simply about commitment, but about those already around the table being prepared to share and discover something of God's kingdom from others. Significantly for me, but probably rather unhelpfully for those stewardship advisors, I had heard a similar phrase – often quoted but seldom referenced – that resonated far more with the work of small, vibrant catholic fresh expressions: I was not interested in moving people from the street to the altar but, 'from the street to the Amen'.

Jesus said to them, 'Therefore every scribe who has been trained for the kingdom of heaven is like the master of a household who brings out of his treasure what is new and what is old.' (Matthew 13.52)

References

Kathleen Burne, 1948, *The Life and Letters of Father Andrew SDC*, London: Mowbrays.

Anscar Chupungco OSB, 1989, *Liturgies of the Future*, New York: Paulist Press.

Joseph Gelineau, 1978, *The Liturgy Today and Tomorrow*, London: Darton Longman and Todd and Paulist Press.

Marty Haugen, 1998, 'Worship and Music: Keeping the People's Song Alive', in a paper delivered to the Evangelical Lutheran Church of America, copyright Marty Haugen; all rights reserved.

Hippolytus, *Apostolic Tradition*, 9:3–5.

Richard Holloway, 1992, *Signs of Glory*, London: Darton, Longman and Todd.

Justin Martyr, *Apologia*, 1:67.

New Patterns for Worship, 2002, London: Church House Publishing.

Pope John Paul II, 1990, Encyclical *'Redemptoris Missio'*, *On the permanent validity of the Church's missionary mandate*.

Alexander Schmemann, 1990, 'The First Nicholas Zernov Memorial Lecture', in Thomas Fisch (ed.), *Liturgy and Tradition*, New York: St Vladimir's Seminary Press.

Andy Warhol, 1975, *The Philosophy of Andy Warhol (From A to B and Back Again)*, New York City: Harcourt, Brace, Jovanovich.

8

Liturgy and Cultural Engagement

PHYLLIS TICKLE

Ours indeed are strange times. To say otherwise would be naïve. It would also be a travesty; for though our times be strange, they are most wondrously so.

Every 500 years, give or take a decade or two, the Church goes through a time of enormous rupture and upheaval which, at least in the words of Episcopalian Bishop Mark Dyer, 'resembles a giant rummage sale more than it does anything else'. While the Bishop's metaphor is undoubtedly intended as a witticism, it nonetheless contains a body of truth that is both historically correct and immediately pertinent. Five hundred years ago, Western Christianity was embroiled in the Great Reformation. Five hundred years prior to that, we were embroiled in the Great Schism. Five hundred years before that, we – or our forebears in the faith and culture – were deep into the throes of a failing world system and the battles of the Council of Chalcedon. (For us as Anglicans, it is of more than passing significance, of course, that this led straight to Gregory the Great and his holy determination to 'convert the Angles'.) Five hundred years before Chalcedon, we passed through what is increasingly being referred to now as the Great Transformation, that time in which all of history groaned and birthed a whole new order.

Were we Jewish, an astute rabbi would probably note that 500 years before the Great Transformation was the Babylonian Captivity and the end of First Temple Judaism and, moreover, that 500 years before Babylon was the end of the Age of the

Judges and the establishment of the royal dynasty out of which Messiah was to come. His or her conclusion would be, in other words, that what we are looking at is a Judaeo-Christian phenomenon. A good sociologist might counter, however, by suggesting that we are not looking at an exclusively religious phenomenon, but rather that each rummage sale has been a full-spectrum, across-the-board, cultural upheaval in which the religious component has been just that – a component. Both the rabbi and the sociologist would be correct.

Our semi-millennial brouhahas always spring from, and involve, every part of human society from economics to domesticity, from systems of political organization to operative conceptualizations of reality. Inevitably, religion becomes the central means for interpreting the chaos of re-formation, just as it becomes the obvious means for structuring a system of adaptations that will grant spiritual and psychological stability to whatever new way of doing things emerges.

As important as it is for us to understand that the Great Emergence – that being the name for the current rummage sale – is but yet another chapter in an on-going saga, it is equally important for us to understand, as twenty-first century Christians, that there are certain historical consistencies that appertain to these times of cataclysmic transition. In none of the previous periods of regrouping and reconfiguring has the dominant or operative form of Christianity been destroyed. It has simply lost hegemony and been forced into accommodation with the world's new socio-cultural and political ways of being. Additionally, in every re-formation Christianity has grown not only geographically and demographically, but – whatever the new or emerging form turned out to be – the Church's theology has grown in depth and breadth.

All our reformations, likewise, have had one central question, and it's always the same one: where now is our authority? For Protestantism and the reformers of the Great Reformation, the answer was Luther's cry of *'sola scriptura, scriptura sola'*. Their religious and spiritual offspring know now that such is no longer a satisfactory, or even a tenable, answer; and so as a culture and as members of a faith, we struggle to find a different one, one that will be both palatable to, and efficacious within, our time and place.

We do not yet have our solution, though around the world, we are working on it, each in his or her own way, in his or her own context. And like those who have pioneered through previous 'new' times, we are looking for our base of authority not only in what we can see lying about us, but also, and perhaps more earnestly, in the artefacts, the *modi operandi* left to us by our forebears. We mine our way through the surviving evidences and forms of what once was and once sustained. This semi-millennial searching of ours rests, of course, on human need more than upon deliberated or even perceived strategy. The propelling assumption is that present times are in chaotic distress, but that there once was a time – 500–600 hundred years ago, 1,000 years ago, 1,500 years ago, somewhere back there – when things made sense and the world was predictable and hospitable. If only we could jump the gathering tsunami of the last half-millennium and return to one of those times of stasis and balance, we would once more find the key to stability and tranquility.

As every one of us knows – when we are thinking, and not just unconsciously reacting – it is incredibly silly, infantile even, to think that there has ever been a time in human history which was heaven on earth, a time that was drenched in good fellowship and logical operation. It is even sillier to think that, in the best of circumstances, we could return to it. But hope springs eternal; or perhaps just instinct does. Certainly in our present era of total tsunami, we have seen, for example, a rampant kind of neo-medievalism sweeping Western culture, presenting sometimes in rather bizarre ways. The rise, and now the holding power, of Goth fashion and Goth lifestyles speak to this. So, too, do the startling sales figures of books like *The Da Vinci Code* which traffic less in literary value than in a popular hunger to know what it was and where it went astray – the 'it' being coherence and cohesion in human affairs.

Popular television shows with names like *Joan of Arcadia*

can hardly be said to reference the contemporary, but rather the previous and earlier. Likewise, the use of chanting-monk actors on television advertisements to sell products as diverse as popular soft drinks and name-brand photocopiers, seeks to tap into the same stream. So, of course, does the pseudo-medieval tone employed in futuristic works of art like *Star Trek* or *Star Wars*, or magical tales like the *Harry Potter* series. The list goes on, but the point remains that we seek a balance that we perceive as having once been. Or, if there was no balance in those inaccurately celebrated times, at least there were the tools for survival. Something there allowed us to get from then to now.

While it may be easy to observe, with a raised eyebrow, our inchoate mining of the past in order to better fashion the future, it would be historically and logically unwise to do so for very long. That is, there is much truth in the old adage that those who do not know history are destined to repeat it. There is also an inherent wisdom in the argument that it is by studying our elders that we discover how to live. This is true not only because we learn from them what not to do, but also, and more powerfully, because we discover in their patterns and values what we want and need to do. We find not only tools for our own survival, but also a stabilizing identity for ourselves as conveyors of cultural heritage.

Robert Webber, the late American theologian, was an as-tute observer and interpreter not only of theoretical theology, but also of practical theology as it was enacted in human lives and ordinary affairs. It was Webber who, in the mid 1970s, coined the phrase 'ancient-future' as a way to name the goi ng-back-in-order-to-go-forward thrust of a Western culture already deep into the Great Emergence (2008, p. 1). Because he was a theologian, Webber focused his perception increas-ingly on the new forms of Christianity emerging out of the West's post-Reformation, post-modern, post-Protestant, post-denominational twentieth century. And long before anyone else really grasped the full implications of what he was saying, it was Webber who was wont to quip in conversation that, 'The best I can tell, we are rapidly racing toward the third century.' He was right, of course, especially in terms of religion. He was also more than right when he published a book, likewise in the mid 1970s, entitled *Evangelicals on the Canterbury Trail.*

It would not be inaccurate to say that almost no one at the time perceived just how prescient Webber really was. It is even possible that he himself did not realize the power with which evangelicals would rush into the Great Emergence. They are marked not only by significant numbers and passion, but also an entrenched, ravenous hunger born of five hundred years of living and worshipping without liturgy, and without liturgical connection to the prior fifteen hundred years of the pre-Protestant Church. But whether Webber fully understood the ramifications of his own insights or not, it would indeed be Canterbury, not Rome, that fed the Great Emergence.

The four streams or tributaries that, in their conjunction, form the river that is Christianity are Roman or Latin Catholicism, Protestantism, Anglicanism, and Orthodoxy. The Great Emergence is removed by a substantial cultural history from Orthodoxy; it is removed by five hundred years of indoctrination from Roman Catholicism; and it is removed by thrust, intention and, if one may say so, protest, from Protestantism, which is too new to sate its hunger. The most available and only acceptable contact with the ancient Church is the last tributary still standing, Anglicanism. This includes Anglo-Catholicism, which is a relatively small, but very significant part of it.

At a practical level, it doesn't matter whether the Great Emergence adopts and adapts historic Anglicanism in overtly Anglican worship and praxis, or whether it simply finds its expression in 'Anglimergent' communities. The end result is the same: Anglicanism is the stream from which our times, and those contained within the next three or four centuries, will drink long and deep.

While the recognition of such a phenomenon may at first be pleasing – and even chauvinistically gratifying – to Anglicans, it does not come without a great price and a huge responsibility. The price is that of allowing a treasured way of discipline and worship to run free of established Episcopal control, and to find its own way in the hands and lives of thousands who have not been so privileged, or so programmed. The responsibility is to hand on and hand out our treasures, like it or not, to all comers, for the furtherance of the Kingdom of God; easily said, painfully achieved. Yet there is in our Anglo-Catholic attic a veritable treasure trove not only of aesthetic and liturgical delights, but also of balms and disciplines, and incarnational practices for the healing of all who may yearn to own them. And it is, of course, the incarnational that, in a field of many operative processes, is the one most sought after by the citizens of the Great Emergence.

To bring into one's body the signs, marks, and diurnal rhythms of one's religion is to form and direct one's innate, human potential for spirituality to some definition outside of the self and the self's experience or purposes. It is, in a sense, to offer constant hospitality to the divine, to furnish one's interior receptively, to grant one's inner being the gracious accoutrements of cleanliness and stability. To assume into one's self the spiritual disciplines of Christianity is also to perfuse the self with the music of common or shared story.

Anglicanism, as a tributary of Christianity, has always so organized its affairs as to be ever mindful of these truths and, as a result, has always been inherently incarnational. It has assumed from the first that a religion that costs nothing, that bears no physical imprint upon the believer, is not a religion, being instead little more than a social habit or a psychological panacea. That recognition and the premises derived from it are central to the developing theology of the Great Emergence, just as both are central to the desires and hungers of the Great Emergence's constituents.

Whether one dates Anglicanism from the first century CE, from the coming to Britain of Augustine, from the Synod of Whitby, or from Henry VIII, it makes little practical difference on the street (though the niceties of it as a question may matter within the seminary or the academy). What matters at an effectual level, in relation to the Great Emergence, is that the most direct and primal way to initially occupy one's own interior, and then to dwell there in safety, is through music; and, given that, what matters is that Celtic music, which shares origin, heritage, and ethos with Anglicanism, has inherent in it a keening, atonal, rhythmic mystery that answers no questions. Rather, it celebrates the space between the inarticulate yet experiencing consciousness, and the supra human. It was entirely predictable, then, that some of the Great Emergence's earliest moves toward finding and pursuing ancient future ways of worship over the closing decades of the twentieth century would be an ardent, thirsty embrace of Celtic music and of its cousin, the music of Taizé. All over the Western world, Christians and want-to-be Christians, seekers and even just shy hopers began attending Celtic masses and meditating with Taizé music long before the century was over. The usually unmentioned fact in this trend is that such masses and seasons of meditation occur more often in Anglican – or Anglo-Catholic or Anglimergent – naves than in any other.

Many an astute person has observed that where there is aesthetic integrity, there also is a concomitant 'something' that is very close to righteousness, even in the mind and soul of an unbeliever. None of Christianity's member-bodies understands this better than does Anglicanism. Music may take one into meditation and a spirit-filled house of the soul, but the soul requires as well a house beyond the parameters of its own skin. Or, to carry the metaphor more consistently, the soul yearns for a neighborhood beyond its own fence-lines. We Anglicans may jest about smells and bells, about passionately bequeathed prayer books and less than illuminating candles, about sneeze-evoking incense and cantankerous altar guilds consumed by a neurotic absorption with fair linen. We may jest, but we jest in self-deprecation, not sincerity. Perhaps we jest as a way not of congratulating ourselves, but of bragging without offending; and well we should. What we have known and practised for centuries, the Great Emergence has learned and is now either borrowing, or joining us in doing.

The Christian spirit, if it is to have formation beyond itself, must have formation in Christian community. This principle makes the choice of which or what community a matter of over-arching importance. The spirit likewise knows, or sometimes merely senses, its own deficiencies; it perceives and interprets its own hungers. Five hundred years of meeting houses without altars, of homilies without pageantry, of prayers with bombast but little grandeur have left the spirit of the post-modern Christian hungering and thirsting; common sense and observation have led that same spirit to rest a while in Anglicanism and to feed there.

But to borrow the outward and deeply satisfying signs of a faith, even of a colourful, aesthetic and acceptable one like Anglicanism, is not enough today. It never was, in fact. More is needed, for even if the spirit is fed, the body still must enter into the conversation. It must be shaped as a house is shaped to the tastes of its occupant, and not the other way around. The ancients knew this, and Christians of the Great Emergence are not so much rediscovering it as they are re-learning how to appreciate it as an operative concept in their lives. They are returning to the ancient disciplines, particularly the liturgical communions, that came into Christianity from Judaism and that have continued to inform the Abrahamic faith.

I am thinking here of tithing, fasting, and the sacred meal by whatever name (be it Eucharist, Communion or the Lord's Supper), and of fixed-hour prayer, Sabbath-keeping, the observance of the liturgical calendar, and pilgrimage. The first three centre around the space that is the human body, its goods and its appetites; the latter four govern or discipline time. The first of these ancient, incarnating disciplines to assume any kind of remarkable or broad presence in emergent practice was fixed-hour prayer, or the daily offices. Eschewing the Roman breviary, some early emergents turned instead to the much less freighted and much more familiar – culturally, if not personally – Book of Common Prayer. From those early adventurers, and from the traction of their growing numbers, came the burgeoning of non-Roman manuals that borrow heavily from the BCP, but are more accessible in form. In fact, some of those manuals have become commercial best-sellers, so great has been the perceived need for them.

The rather broad return to the Daily Offices by Christians who were not liturgical by birth or heritage, but who were definitively emergent, led in the last century to a rather gentle, but steady increase of interest in the BCP itself, and to a new acceptance of 'rote' prayer as a means of connecting to a body of fellow Christians in other places and other times. The prayer book, in that stance, becomes not just a means of ordering worship, but also a means of transport.

But once one begins to dip into the Book of Common Prayer and/or to set one's foot inside an Anglican nave, one is inevitably nudged into the recognition that there is an ordering of time here that is neither secular nor physical. Probably no part of Anglicanism has had a more subtle but informing impact on the ordinary emerging Christian, than the current rediscovery of the liturgical calendar. The cry of 'Why were we never told this before?' is not only omnipresent, but it is also almost always raised with some degree of resentment and belligerence.

No small consequence of the rediscovery of the liturgical year has been, of course, a rediscovery of saints and martyrs as acceptable objects not only of conversation, but also of reverent consideration. What was it that once upon a distant time made a saint, or formed an early Church Father, or sustained a martyr? Who were they, and why were they? And how can I/we find such force of Christian character as to inhabit time in their way? These are not only legitimate questions; they are also the rallying cry of Christians who have discovered within themselves a hunger for heroes and heroines of the soul, a hunger that will not be assuaged by anything less than informed recognition of heritage.

The other, immediately visible consequence of dipping one's toe into Anglican prayer books and Anglican naves is a passionate appreciation for both the Sabbath and the sacred meal as beautiful things to be embraced with joyful hearts. There is inherent in Anglicanism, also, a kind of generosity that acknowledges the diversity of humanity and receives into itself with good humor the odd, the outré, sometimes even the somewhat aberrant. While one may regard such a stance as Christian hospitality, it has the feel of grace that deals more in compassion than in doctrine. In a time of upheaval, when all things are in motion, such stability and predictability of acceptance make the previously unfamiliar, very attractive.

All of this is to say in particular the same thing that Robert Webber once said in general, albeit with two significant adjustments. One is a matter of change in Webber's wording, and the other is an expansion in interpretation. It is not evangelicals who are on the Canterbury trail; rather, it is a much larger company. It is the Christians of the Great Emergence who, in large part, are either on the Canterbury trail or are absorbing and re-employing the characteristics, spirituality, and practices of pilgrims.

As for interpretation, one must be careful to note that all of this should not be understood as some grand explosion of Anglicanism. That would not be accurate, nor is that the conclusion of my message. None of us can know now – or for several decades, I should imagine – just what emergent/emerging/emersion Christianity will finally mature into. The only sureties are that it will mature and that, as it does, Anglicanism will be the stream of Christian thought and heritage that will influence and inform it more deeply than any other.

Pray God, then, that our long Anglican history of hospitality will indeed not desert us now, and that we shall find the grace to welcome those who come, and to embrace and support, even to the point of self-sacrifice, those who wish simply to take.

Reference

Robert Webber, 2008, *Ancient-Future Worship: Proclaiming and Enacting God's Narrative*, Grand Rapids: Baker Books.

9

Alternative Worship and the Story of Visions in York

SUE WALLACE

The story of Visions starts an embarrassingly long time ago (before some of our younger members were even born), with a one-off event. Back in the summer of 1989 an outreach event was happening in York city centre, featuring a video link-up with Billy Graham. While this was going on, in a dark corner of a different York church, a group of people wondered what opportunities there might be for those who didn't want to go to York Minster and hear an American preacher – the sort of people who generally didn't show up at church. They assembled a team and, for one month, ran a nightclub in an old warehouse as a venue for bands to play at, and a place for artists to meet. It was at this point that I came on board, in one of those random, life-changing events: someone shoved a pink form into my hand at the end of a church service and said, 'You're a student. You're not doing much this summer. Do this.' So I did!

And, as often happens at large, city-wide events, new friendships were born and new connections were made. After the event a small group of people began meeting to pray and share their dreams. They wanted to explore mission, culture and community, and to dream up a way of reaching those who were happy to go to that nightclub, but not to turn up at a church service. Originally, this bunch of dreamers were members of different churches in the city centre, but they decided to attach themselves to St Michael le Belfrey because the vicar at the time, Graham Cray, was an expert in mission and culture.

And so the years of our pilgrimage began. We spent the first two simply building community, praying, getting to know the nightlife in York, and wondering what we should do next. We also commuted frequently to the 'Nine O'clock Service' at St Thomas Church in Crookes, Sheffield. We were amazed by their multimedia services, and the mixing of ancient forms of catholic prayer and chant with Goth and dance culture.

Eventually we realized there was a hunger inside us to start a service of our own, and so in August 1991 the first Visions service was born (although at that time we called it Warehouse, after the old warehouse where we first met one another). Initially it happened on a monthly basis. In those days the service was neither very catholic nor very contemplative; it had a twenty-minute praise session to loud dance music, followed by a twenty-minute sermon! Over time we realized that this approach wasn't really feeding us spiritually. We began to explore Celtic spirituality, which felt deeply appropriate to us as the church building we used, erected in 687 CE, sits on the historic site where Saint Cuthbert blessed the city of York. We investigated Cuthbert further by going on pilgrimage to Lindisfarne. We took inspiration from the way the Celtic saints built community by reaching out to their culture and mixing with the people. So we too mixed with the people of York: we did visuals for nightclubs, danced alongside other clubbers, listened to their stories, and stayed open about our Christian faith. In those days we envisaged the church quickly becoming full of converted clubbers, but this never really happened. What did happen, though, was that those who were antagonistic towards Christians and Christianity changed their opinions a little. 'The Christians, oh they do great visuals,' was the comment we kept hearing. We took this as great praise, considering some of the awful things people were saying about Christians when we first started working in clubs.

A couple of years after our first service we began to feel a sense of hunger to share communion together, and so we began a new monthly communion service, alongside the other service. This was a much more mellow and contemplative service, with Bible meditation, story, and images accompanied by a constant gentle wash of ambient music. As no members of Visions were ordained at the time we had to ask local clergy to come and celebrate communion with us. At first we saw this as a disadvantage, but it actually became a wonderful opportunity to build friendships with, and gain the support of, the local clergy. It was in the context of this communion service that we first began to explore creative prayer; we soon learned it was a powerful way of connecting to God. We began to explore as many different ways of praying as we could find, drawing on many different Christian traditions along the way. We went on pilgrimage to Chartres, France, and walked the labyrinth there. We then built one of our own, opening it one Sunday each month, lighting candles, playing plainchant on the stereo and simply allowing people to use the space for prayer.

Soon after this we entered our 'wilderness years', as they became known. The infamous and deeply public scandal that happened with the Nine O'clock Service affected many alternative worship groups at the time. In York, we had a crisis of confidence, especially on the mission front, for how could we promote ourselves when people made connections between fresh expressions of worship and abusive practices? The scandal also shattered all the friendships and trust we had carefully nurtured within the clubbing community. We had to run around apologising to people for ever having invited them to come to Sheffield with us (which was our only, and tenuous, connection with the scandal). Yet we found comfort and inspiration during that terrible time from two sources. First, the communion of the saints and the stories of the heroes, old and new, who had suffered far worse trials than we were going through at the time: St Francis, Oscar Romero, Thérèse of Lisieux, Maximilian Kolbe, and others. We shared some of those stories in our service themes, and as we listened to the trials and achievements of the saints, hope began to spring up inside us again. The other source of inspiration at that time was the Orthodox

Church. We developed some lasting friendships with Orthodox clergy, in person and on the Internet, and the depth of their spirituality, having weathered storms much tougher than ours, gave us the strength to continue.

Through all the years of experimenting with different methods of prayer and worship, we gradually found a pattern that worked for us, and actually it was a variation on the old 'hymn-sandwich' idea. The hymns, secular songs, chants, home-grown songs, prayers, Bible readings, liturgies old and new, stories and meditations were all mixed together over a seamlessly woven musical background, provided by the church DJ. There was variety in the mix, and yet it didn't feel disconnected because the music held it all together. Thankfully, the Performing Right Society (PRS) allow churches to play secular music in worship services free of charge, and we therefore had a huge variety of instrumental tracks to choose from for our services. By this time, we had also bought our beanbags, which, although they sound a bit minor and random at first, are actually a rather important part of the mix. It is amazing how many visitors comment on the beanbags more than any other aspect of the service, because, at last, they have something comfortable to sit on in church! Later, as we got older, we brought in sofas which also helped people relax in God's presence, without the distraction of uncomfortable pews or folding chairs (some of which can be quite painful!).

In the mid to late 1990s, Visions began to follow the lectionary, which gave us a sense of continuity and connection with the wider Church whilst also challenging us to confront difficult subjects we might otherwise have avoided. Having the Bible readings prepared so far in advance also made forward planning much easier, and we found that there was plenty of scope in the readings for us to be creative. We began to collect together some of the multi-sensory prayer ideas we had used in our services, and I was looking for a publisher when I bumped into a friend who offered to take them in to the Scripture Union offices. In one of those bizarre 'God coincidences', this happened to be just at a time when they were looking for a prayer book that was different from the usual sort. 'Multi-sensory Prayer' was published in 2000, and was followed later by two more books. A fourth book will also be published in 2009.

One of the things that sometimes puzzles people about Visions is the fact that we are attached to a large charismatic evangelical church. However, a visitor to Visions expecting a typical charismatic evangelical teaching service will get rather a shock! We differ stylistically in our use of liturgy, chants, incense, imagery and creative prayer. Our relationship with our parent Church remains healthy as long as we still value and teach Scripture (although this can be done in any way we wish, such as Ignatian meditation). We have found over time that Visions has unique gifts to offer back to our spiritual parents, and that they too have things to teach us, particularly in the area of healing prayer. Visions has also been deeply inspired by the pioneering artists at St Michael's who nurtured the arts in the days when they were still frowned upon in evangelical circles. The same people also fostered Christian community in a world that has forgotten the meaning of it.

The final section of our story is the part that is just beginning. Visions had been going for so long that I'd forgotten what it's like to start something new, and to feel that tingle of anticipation when faced with a completely blank sheet of paper. We are now, however, experiencing this all over again, having recently started a new project in partnership with York Minster called 'Transcendence: An Ancient-Future Mass'.

There were several sources of inspiration for the service, one being rather random. In 2007 St Cuthbert's roof needed major repairs, meaning that Visions had to move house for a while. We asked York Minster if they would allow us to meet there for a while, and they very generously gave us the use of their crypt. We have since realized that by meeting in the Minster we reach far more people than at St Cuthbert's. We also realize that the informality of Visions simply didn't work so well in the Minster space. Another piece of inspiration for this service was my MA research in mission and culture. I discovered that many people in York value the Minster as a spiritual place, visiting it regularly; curiously even some atheists claim to sense something spiritual there.

So, when we moved back to St Cuthbert's we investigated starting a new fresh expression in the Minster. It was to be a genuine piece of teamwork between Visions and the Minster. Transcendence is very formal and traditional in some ways: we use Common Worship Order 1, we wear robes, we have processions complete with thurifer and crucifer, we sing hymns, and all is generally set to a Latin Mass, sometimes sung by the amazing Minster song men. On the other hand, the hymns are sung to trip hop or ambient dance backings, and the building is dark and candlelit, with moving images on every available space. The congregation can sit on chairs or, if they wish, they can lie down and relax on rugs and cushions. One of the most popular elements of the service is the chance to move around the building, normally to visit prayer stations set up in different chapels during a time of creative prayer. We started Transcendence with two trial services in October and November 2007, inviting people to tell us if they thought we were on the right track. We were completely blown away by the warmth and enthusiasm of the responses! It is a much more traditional service than anything I would have imagined doing ten years ago, and yet somehow, because it is reinterpreted within a multimedia framework, it really works! I think it's because the familiarity of the traditional Mass structure enables people to cope when something unusual and creative happens. We have also found that some spiritual seekers are put off when everything is very new – when it isn't how they imagine church to be.

Another wonderful thing about being in the Minster is that the building itself attracts spiritual seekers. Many people just wander in to have a look around, sometimes popping into services, or hovering on the edges like an audience. The task of simply setting up for Transcendence has also become a joy rather than a chore. As people see the coloured lights and projections going up, they often ask, 'Are you setting up for a concert?' This gives us the chance to explain what we are doing. Sometimes people take out their cameras and take snaps of us, and we become tourist attractions ourselves. On one occasion, as we were setting up, I actually explained what the service of Holy Communion was all about to a Chinese tourist. For this individual the whole concept was a totally new discovery, and all the work involved in that month's Transcendence was totally worth it for that one amazing conversation.

It is fantastic that we can use York Minster; it is such a unique place, with much already happening mission-wise. We have also had the wonderful privilege of drawing on the liturgical and musical skill of some members of the Minster community. Each time we have done it, the service has been a little different, and each time we have felt like we are exploring new territory. However, the framework has always been a familiar and ancient one, reinterpreted so as be accessible, and to impact those who have never experienced it before. Visions has certainly come a long way since our initial conversations in the warehouse in 1989, but the constant process of both pilgrimage and 'remixing', keeps us true to our calling. The future for us, at least at the moment, seems to be ancient.

10

U2charist

PAIGE BLAIR

It's Sunday night, 3 August 2008. At St George's Episcopal
Church in York, Maine we're celebrating the third anniversary
of our first U2charist, honouring what has emerged from the
passions and gifts of one small church, and spread around the
world. Faithful people praise God's name, and give thanks for
the gift given through Jesus Christ in the name of love. A fire
is lit in our bellies to serve the most vulnerable and needy, and
achieve the Millennium Development Goal (MDG) of eradicat-
ing extreme poverty from the world – and all this to the beat of
the greatest rock band in history.

Over the past three years more than 700 churches have contacted St George's, seeking support and consultation for hosting their own U2charist services. More than 150 have gone on
to do so, in places as diverse as Lubbock, Texas; Cape Town,
South Africa; Walla Walla, Washington; and Hong Kong. They
represent denominations as diverse as Presbyterian, Methodist, Free Evangelical, United Church of Christ, Lutheran,
Roman Catholic, and various flavours of Anglican. All in all
more than 20,000 people have attended U2charists, and together have raised over $250,000 USD to help fight extreme
poverty and the global AIDS epidemic. The offerings have gone
to organizations as diverse as the ecclesiology and geography
of the services themselves: Five Talents International, Oxfam,
Mercy Corps, Bread for Life, CARE International, Bread for
the World, Heifer International, KIVA, Episcopal Relief and
Development, The Church World Service, and the Millennium

Village Project. Additionally, many local AIDS Service Organizations have received assistance as they engage the MDGs closer to home through HIV/AIDS prevention and education.

While the numerical results of the ministry over three years have been remarkable, what has been more transforming from my view are the intangibles. Countless people from around the world have come to a new awareness of their connectedness to each other, realizing, as Bono said, that 'In the Global Village, distance no longer decides who is your neighbor, and "Love thy neighbor" is not advice, it's a command' (Assayas, 2005).

Come to think of it, even the intangibles become tangible. The most recent story of such awareness and transformation may be the most powerful: the arrival in August 2008 of 15-month-old Ethiopian, Augustine 'Gus' Fitsum Beecher, who was adopted by Tom and Jane Beecher. Tom and Jane were inspired to enfold Gus into their family by their involvement in the U2charist Team and other MDG ministries in our parish. Wonderfully, Gus was able to attend the third anniversary of the U2charist, his parents having played leading roles in its story from the earliest chapters.

The story itself is best told in terms of emergence, for the U2charist literally emerged from St George's, much as it emerged in other communities around the world. The publicity that arose from the U2charist allowed us to connect with Dutch pastor Jan Andries DeBoer, whose 'U2deinst' emerged synchronously with our U2charist at St George's. In contexts near and far, it was as if the Spirit drew the U2charist out of us, by engaging our passions, our history, and our yearnings.

When U2's 2004 release 'How to Dismantle an Atomic Bomb' arrived, the fans at St George's were thrilled that it maintained the lyrical quality and overt spirituality of their earlier work. The band repeatedly came up in conversation around the parish at vestry meetings, pastoral care classes, and coffee hours. And the subject was not merely how good a sound the Edge got out of his guitar, or the driving, reliable quality of Adam Clayton's bass playing. Instead, we were talking about how U2 had long been a spiritual resource for us, particularly in our earlier lives when the Church had not been as strong a presence for us. We remembered singing at the top of our lungs 'Gloria', 'Pride (In the Name of Love)', and 'I Still Haven't Found What I'm Looking For', and turning our cars or dorm rooms into private chapels. In this way, U2's last two albums felt a bit like a reunion with dear spiritual friends. Soon, the *conversation* became the conversation – and we started to ask what the ubiquitousness of U2 would mean for us at St George's.

One morning in the spring of 2005, I was working on an icon of the Beloved Disciple, which was to be an ordination present for my associate. U2's *Greatest Hits 1980–1990* was playing loudly in the background, and when 'I Will Follow' came on, I unconsciously put down my brush and pushed back the chair from the dining room table where I was working. I began dancing and singing at the top of my lungs, and was overcome by a powerful experience of the Holy Spirit. For some time my clergy colleagues and I had been talking about what a U2 Eucharist might look like. As the last guitar strains faded I realized it was time to stop talking about it, and finally bring this powerful music out of the private chapels of our automobiles, Walkmen and iPods and into the nave of the church.

When I floated the idea with the U2 fans among my parishioners, they were universally enthusiastic. So my associate Steve Godfrey and I, along with one of our youth, Eliza Duquette, brainstormed one afternoon – how would we make this music happen? Would it be live, or recorded? At the end of the conversation, 16-year-old Eliza began dancing from one foot to another, chanting, 'U2 ... Eucharist. U2 ... Eucharist. U2charist!' Eliza's father, Bob, was our sign-maker, and so U2charist it was.

Using U2's music in liturgy was not a new idea. My first such experience was in 1990 at Boston University in Boston, Massachusetts. Our chaplain, the Revd Jep Streit, was a U2 fan. One Sunday he found irresistible the presence of Psalm 40 in the weekly propers. He came to chapel that Sunday night with the requisite pita bread and a tape deck with the album *War* queued up. When singing the psalm, we all intoned, 'I waited patiently for the Lord; he inclined and heard my cry. He lifted me up out of the pit, out of the miry clay. And I will sing ... Sing a new song ... I will sing ... sing a new song. How long, to sing this song?'

The chances of our U2charist landing on a Sunday in which Psalm 40 was the appointed psalm seemed pretty slim. We felt that if this was going to work, it had to fit with the weekly propers, and not some handpicked collection of readings that seemed to fit the music we wanted to play. So, over the next few weeks the nascent U2charist Team surveyed their CD collections and listened to their favorite U2 songs while commuting, cleaning the house, and going for walks. They listened for the songs with the most overt spiritual content (all of U2's songs have spiritual content, but in order to appease the few, inevitable sceptics we wanted the spirituality to be bold and irrefutable). Bringing together our song ideas, we discussed where in the service the songs belonged: as a prelude, postlude, Gloria, communion hymn, offertory, or closing hymn? Perhaps as a sung collect to the prayers, or as a response to God's generous forgiveness in the confession and absolution?

In addition, I emailed my clergy colleagues in the larger Church and asked for their ideas: had they held a U2 service, or only dreamed of one, and what was their play list? They shared their ideas generously, and from one of these colleagues I learned that Sarah Dylan Breuer, with the good people of Baltimore Maryland's 'Church Without Walls', had indeed held a service called 'eU2charist'. *Get Up Off Your Knees*, a collection of sermons based on U2's catalog, had just been published and Breuer had been a contributor. From the 'Church Without Walls' we received affirmation of our desire to use 'When Love Comes to Town' in response to the Confession and Absolution – a part of the U2charist liturgy at St George's that we have been unable to change due to popular demand. After just three years, and already it's 'we've always done it this way'. How quickly that happens, even in the context of contemporary liturgy!

Together, with suggestions and affirmations from many enthusiastic quarters, we designed our first U2charist service. We decided to use recorded music because we have no an established praise band that could lead the music convincingly. PowerPoint software became our disc jockey and liturgical timing genius. We took the opportunity it provided to add pictures to illustrate some of the songs. Although many churches over these three years have done a wholesale rewrite of the liturgy, in our particular parish context we used approved liturgical texts, beginning with *Enriching Our Worship*. Not wanting to capitalize on U2's popularity, we made the decision to split the offering between TASO Uganda, an AIDS service organization with which Bono's DATA had a relationship, and our local AIDS service organization, AIDS Response Seacoast.

As St George's does whenever we think we have Good News to share, we sent out press releases to the local media. A reporter from the *Portsmouth Herald*, Emily Wiggin, interviewed me for an article that ran on the Thursday before the service. We talked about U2's history as a band of Christians, ever using Scripture and traditional theological and spiritual content in their lyrics. I recalled U2's history of making an offering of their gifts and lives to Almighty God, particularly through their efforts with Amnesty International and participation in Live Aid and other anti-hunger efforts. She asked for specific biblical references, and I shared those that would be part of the service that Sunday night. She concluded her article by saying not only would she never listen to U2 in quite the same way, but she might even have to pick up the Bible and see what they were singing about. That alone felt like victory for God.

The service itself was more successful than we could have imagined. We expected about 60 people, and had 130 (our space seats 100 comfortably). We figured on mostly friends from St George's, and instead had a house two-thirds full of visitors. We figured on mostly Gen Xer's and some Millennials, but were delighted that the ages ranged between 7 months and 70 years. We are in a seaside resort town, and on that last Sunday in July, God graced us with a drizzly afternoon and evening. People wanted somewhere to go, and so they came to St George's and sang praises to Almighty God. They learned about the movement to make poverty history, and how they could do as U2 has done, and offer their gifts to God for the healing of the world. As the service concluded they danced and sang 'I Will Follow' at the top of their lungs.

All along I figured that we'd do another U2charist, perhaps in the dark months of winter when cabin fever sets in and we all need some inspiration. However, the overwhelming consensus was to do it much sooner, in the Fall. And so we did, and this time the field organizer for the ONE Campaign, Julie Heinz, attended and spoke about the Millennium Development Goals.

Meanwhile, reporter Emily Wiggins' article found its way to U2 blogs around the Internet, and soon we were inundated with requests from other churches around the world: what was our play list? Would we be willing to share? How did we negotiate with Universal Music? Some churches began asking us to take the service on the road, and so we did. The first such service was at Grace Church, in Providence, Rhode Island. Ray Henry, a reporter from the Associated Press (AP) attended that service, and wrote what we appreciatively call 'The article that was read around the world', appearing in papers as diverse as *The Times* in the UK, the *Scotsman* and the *Uzbekestani Times*. It resulted in radio interviews with the BBC World Service, BBC Belfast and KFOG in San Francisco. As that AP article ran, we began to get more requests for information from other countries such as Holland, Mexico, Hong Kong, New Zealand, Australia, the UK, as well as a host of requests from across the United States.

The consulting we did, and media contact we had, always involved educating and empowering congregations and individuals for the work of engaging the MDGs. These are eight goals designed to reduce extreme poverty by the year 2015. They are not the same as the development programmes of our grandparents' generation, which often assumed that the Western developed world knew what was right and best for those in need – the dollars often being allocated to allies in the Cold War effort to 'stem the Red tide', rather than helping those most in need, in the most effective ways. Instead, the MDGs are about empowering local communities, encouraging transparency, and fighting corruption. They address the root causes of poverty such as a lack of education, diseases that hamper economic growth, gender discrimination, abuse of the environment and unfair trade arrangements.

When praying through the Millennium Development Goals, many (such as Episcopalians for Global Reconciliation) felt a clear resonance with Christ's mandate in Matthew 25.36:

I was hungry and you fed me,
I was thirsty and you gave me a drink,
I was homeless and you gave me a room,
I was shivering and you gave me clothes,
I was sick and you stopped to visit,
I was in prison and you came to me.
(The Message)

Nearly a year after the first U2charist at St George's, the Episcopal Church held its 76th General Convention in Columbus, Ohio. Episcopalians for Global Reconciliation asked me to coordinate their convention presence, and to include a U2charist service as part of that. Having invited all the bishops and deputies, we received 375 positive responses, and so prepared bread and wine for 400. In reality, 800 attended, and many more were turned away. That service was a symbolic embodiment of global reconciliation, with well-known conservatives and liberals from all across the Church praying, celebrating, blessing God's name. That day we made incarnate the lyrics of the U2 song, 'One': 'We're one, but we're not the same, we've got to carry each other ... One...' The MDGs were the heart of conversation at that General Convention. As we prayed about how to be in relationship with the rest of the Anglican Communion, they shone as a beacon for how we should relate with the world in Christ's name.

Ultimately, the MDGs were voted the number one mission priority for the next three years in the Episcopal Church, and, as a consequence, many parishes and dioceses found themselves in need of ways to communicate their importance. Again, we were overwhelmed by requests for consultation, and invitations to take the U2charist on the road.

Eventually, various members of St George's U2charist Team took on public leadership roles, such as designing PowerPoint slideshows, preaching, and serving as U2charist consultants and project managers for other churches. And then, under the leadership of Eric Hopkins – who is responsible for some of our most compelling PowerPoint displays and sermon illustrations – the Team took the service on the road. In that moment I knew that the U2charist movement had reached a self-sustaining maturity, independent of my leadership and involvement. The movement's local emergence was complete: with God's help I had taught and cajoled and trained and encouraged myself out of a job!

Gradually, as the word continued to spread, other churches began serving as consultants too. When the donated offerings topped $250,000, it became very clear that this movement had grown well beyond what we could track. Praise God! Recall the icon of the Beloved Disciple I had been working on that spring morning in 2005, when I was so inspired by U2's 'I Will Follow'. We used that icon to illustrate the PowerPoint for 'Pride in the Name of Love'. Eventually that same Beloved Disciple began appearing in pictures from news stories about U2charists for which we had not directly consulted. The Beloved Disciple was now a citizen of the world, and the U2charist movement in its global incarnation had truly emerged, reaching a maturity that no longer depended entirely on us.

Since then we have continued to hold our own U2charists quarterly at St George's, and we still occasionally take the service on the road. Several times a week we receive inquiries and consultation requests from people interested in bringing the U2charist to their own church. Because of the media attention, Archbishop Thomas Cranmer and Martin Luther appeared in the same article as Bono, the Edge, Adam Clayton and Larry Mullen Jr. U2charist has also helped promote ideas such as the translation of Anglican worship into the vernacular, and of liturgy being the work of the people, with related articles appearing in *USA Today*, the TV news magazine and *Nightline*. And vitally, of course, God's call to serve those most in need, as articulated in the Millennium Development Goals, was greatly elevated. Regardless of theological bent or political inclinations, the MDGs enable us to work towards a more hopeful and blessed future for our neighbours near and far.

Having just received Gus Fitsum Beecher home, we're wondering what will emerge next. What passions and interests and gifts will God draw out of us? In what way will God call us to work together for the healing and reconciliation of the world? What gifts are we uniquely equipped to offer the Church? What will the next incarnation of the work of the people look or sound like?

And so we wait, and pray, and continue to offer ourselves, as Christ did, as U2 does, as millions of faithful people around the world do every day when they awake and make an oblation of themselves to God. 'Take these hands. Teach them what to carry ...'

Reference

Michka Assayas, *Ode magazine*, November 2005, viewed on 13 January 2009 at http://www.odemagazine.com/doc/28/bono_wants_you

Episcopal Church, Standing Liturgical Commission, 1997, *Enriching our Worship: Supplemental Liturgical Materials*, New York: Church Publishing.

11

Feig, and Growing into the Tradition

Or, Growing Out Of, and Into, the Cathedral
(and thereby into the tradition)

MICHAEL VOLLAND

People often ask what 'feig' means, guessing that it has Celtic,
or perhaps Scandinavian roots – as if you could buy it in Ikea.
It's not Celtic or Scandinavian, and it doesn't mean anything at
all – not in English anyway. Feig means *us* – the members of
a small Christian community that is taking root in the centre
of Gloucester. We avoided giving ourselves a name for the first
year of our existence – what would have been the point? We
were simply a roomful of people trying to follow and worship
Christ with integrity; that kind of thing doesn't require a name.
The invitation in 2007 to host an act of worship at the Greenbelt Festival, however, did. We quickly discovered that names
are a surprisingly tricky business, and that naming something
can seem to limit it – to define its shape too restrictively, or
mark its boundaries too permanently; if we are *this* then we
are not *that*. None of us was happy about this rigidity, and
very aware that words are loaded with baggage – you can never
be sure that what you intend to convey is what others will
understand. Having struggled with the matter for some time
we opted for a made-up word, free from baggage, to which
we could give meaning. The fact that feig makes people think
of things Celtic obviously leads to certain unintended assumptions of what we're about, but how can this ever be completely
avoided? The name stuck and it works for us.

By way of explanation of the subtitle of this chapter I will sketch the story of feig's evolution, a process of trial and error in finding the form best suited to surviving and thriving in the environment in which we found ourselves. It all began with the multiplication of singled-celled ideas in the rich primeval soup of an Episcopal mind, a job-seeking Ordinand, a cathedral Chapter, and a city centre.

During my penultimate term at theological college I received a message from my Principal saying that I was to phone the Bishop of Tewkesbury as soon as possible. I rang him immediately and listened as he outlined an idea for a pioneer curacy in Gloucester. The job would entail being attached to the cathedral as assistant curate while pioneering a fresh expression of church in the city centre. Although Christians have been pioneering things for many centuries, up until that point – as far as I was aware – the Church of England had never ordained a deacon with the specific designation 'pioneer minister'. I hadn't undertaken pioneer training, knew nothing about cathedrals, and wasn't even entirely sure where Gloucester was. I was intrigued, nevertheless, and, to cut a long appointment-story short, I accepted the job. But accepting a job that no one else had done before meant finding workable answers to a lot of questions. What was the intended outcome of the initiative? How would we go about achieving this? How would I finish my continuing ministerial education? How would I gain experience of the Occasional Offices? Who would oversee my priestly formation? To whom would I be accountable? What would be my relationship to the city deanery? Who would be my training incumbent? Who would provide wisdom and guidance as far as the pioneering was concerned? Hours of thinking and discussing, of drafting and re-drafting, resulted in answers that provided enough confidence to get the project off the ground. However, like anything new and unknown, the proof of the pudding would ultimately be in the eating. My training incumbent (the canon-missioner) and I would have to get on with the job in hand and continue attending to tough questions as we went along.

In the weeks after my ordination, my incumbent and I gathered together a council of reference to discuss our options. It was already a given that this initiative was about pioneering a new community for people who struggled with traditional forms of church. It was also assumed that whatever emerged would view itself as part of the one, holy, catholic and apostolic Church and not as a free, independent expression of church. Beyond this we agreed that we wanted to emphasize growing church *with* people and not *for* them, and that we would focus on the journey and not a predetermined destination. We resolved not to limit ourselves to building a gathered congregation, recognizing that in urban settings people belong to a variety of fluid networks. In order to engage effectively in mission we felt the best approach would be the construction of a small, dynamic, core community who would have a high level of commitment to one another and to God, and a firm grasp of the experimental nature of the project. This core would draw together others – both Christians and seekers – to collaborate on a rhythm of events that would facilitate growth in faith and be a springboard from which discipleship would occur. We envisaged making contact with a range of seekers, deepening relationships with these people through regular contact, and drawing on a variety of Christian traditions to enable robust exploration of the faith. We imagined that the end result, in terms of mission, would be a kind of perpetual outward motion rather than a gathering of converts and church-shoppers into a 'fresh expressions' barn of our own construction.

Being grafted into the cathedral's rhythm of life and worship meant, among other things, that I rapidly developed an awareness of the potential of the ancient building as a resource for mission. As well as having a powerful sense of being a *thin* place, ripe for stimulating spiritual exploration, the cathedral occupies a central position in the life of the city both geographically and emotionally. As I began to meet people of no faith, hesitant faith, and tried-and-tested faith, and to work towards carving out something approaching church, it became apparent that the cathedral would naturally occupy a large space in our common lives. As the community started to take shape, we realized there would be little point in trying to secure our own building; we would locate our community in various homes, and when a bigger or more evocative venue was needed we would use the cathedral.

From the beginning the communal worship of the emerging community veered naturally towards the contemplative. Times of prayerful silence, meditation on words of Scripture, music, film and other works of art, along with simple liturgies and rituals marked the hours after lively meals around candle-lit kitchen tables. As the core community increased in size, we experimented with hosting days of contemplative prayer, using the hidden chapels in the cathedral, and on one occasion spreading prayer-stations throughout the entire building. The music of Philip Roderick – the Anglican priest who started the Quiet Garden Movement and who now facilitates Contemplative Fire – has been a powerful influence on us. Philip plays a Hang drum – a unique instrument that looks a little like two woks welded together. I heard him play it for the first time at a *Blah* conference in London in 2007, and was so impressed that I brought his CD back to the community. His profound music can be heard weaving in and out at many of our gatherings; we find it especially evocative when played quietly as the continuous background soundtrack to our Eucharist services. It was a huge privilege, therefore, when Philip and his wife agreed to play their Hang drums at an event we were to stage at the cathedral in the summer of 2008 in conjunction – for the second time – with the Greenbelt Festival. Because of our proximity to the venue at Cheltenham Racecourse, I offered to organize a pre-Greenbelt meal for assorted writers, thinkers, speakers and participants in emerging and fresh expressions of church. Although the meal took place in the cathedral it had been conceived and planned by our ragtag community working out of a living room. To say that it was deeply encouraging to have almost one hundred people from across the UK and the United States turn up is a huge understatement. Whilst the food, wine, fertile conversations and opportunity to forge new friendships were all fantastic, the most enriching thing by far for the members of feig was the act of contemplative worship that took place during the last hour of our time together. We directed people into the cavernous Norman nave, which had been emptied of chairs. The only light came from candles placed in a circle around a huge canvass painted with a copy of the Chartres labyrinth. Having explained how to use the labyrinth and led us in a simple, expectant prayer, Philip and his wife sat to one side and produced wonderful, soaring sounds from their Hang drums. Those gathered in the candlelight either walked the labyrinth or sat in prayerful silence, many experiencing a heightened awareness of the immanence of God. This powerful experience effected personal and corporate transformation, and served to renew feig's commitment to contemplative worship as a resource for mission and evangelism in the emerging culture.

I have stated that the feig community grew out of the cathedral; I say this because I am rooted in the cathedral as the assistant curate, and it was my task to pioneer something new. But because the Dean and Chapter have been hugely supportive of my efforts, and permission-giving in terms of our use of the building, and because the cathedral functions as such a powerful icon of feig's membership of the Church-catholic, it has become a natural home for us. In many ways we might now say that feig has grown *into* the cathedral. As we have done so we have begun to explore aspects of the Christian tradition that many of us had been living in ignorance of – hence the bracketed remark in my subtitle. The engagement with the cathedral, both as building and living community, has enabled members of feig to discover the richness of rhythms of prayer, of liturgy, ritual, silence, and engagement with environmental and social justice issues that have typically been associated with the catholic and contemplative traditions. These have enriched our own spiritual journeys and are enabling us to connect with those who are interested in exploring the Christian faith.

Feig's journey has been a voyage of discovery, not unlike St Brendan's, in which we have pushed out from the shore in a small open boat and allowed ourselves to be directed by the wind of the Spirit. Our journey in the open sea of the catholic and contemplative traditions has taken us into waters foreign to us, teaching us valuable lessons that will travel with us into the unknown.

12

Contemplative Fire: Creating a Community of Christ at the Edge

PHILIP RODERICK AND TESSA HOLLAND

The Lineage: the inheritance of the saints

What draws together tradition and improvisation, conviviality and hiddenness, service and solitude? Contemplative Fire, as a dispersed and eucharistic community of Christ, seeks to hold in creative tension these and other apparent polarities. They are quintessential paradoxes that have been felt, lived, wrestled with and reflected upon since the time of Jesus and the earliest Christian communities.

Contemplative Fire, as its name suggests, seeks to integrate the opposites. Born from within a parish ministry, and drawing from the well of wisdom across the centuries, it is an adventure, a risk, a passion to be shared. Our lineage is the sacred stream that weaves itself through Jesus and the disciples, through oral tradition and biblical text, through the radiance of acclaimed and incognito saints.

As Contemplative Fire responds to Jesus' invitation to 'put out into the deep and let down your nets for a catch', so we also seek to honour and dialogue with the biblical, patristic, monastic and missional lineage, which spread from the great cities of Jerusalem, Alexandria, Antioch, Athens and Rome, through the deserts of Palestine, Syria and Egypt and along the ancient sea-routes from the Eastern Mediterranean to the Celtic ports and promontories.

Inspired by pioneers of faith and the exemplars of holiness down through the ages, our understanding is that the body of the earth, the human body and a body of people gathered in celebration of the presence of God, can be transparent to the grace and illumination of the Holy Spirit, just as is the body of Christ. Scripture and sacrament, spiritual ascesis and service all converge on the fulfilling of personhood as we recognize in each other 'not strangers but pilgrims'.

This 'community of Christ at the edge' has a contemplative and apostolic focus. Such a focus finds expression first in the revisiting and refashioning of a Christ-centred mysticism that incorporates both the beauty of nature and practical compassion; secondly, in the deconstructing and reconstructing of language, symbol and sacrament for use in an accessible, reflective and inclusive liturgy and theology; thirdly, in the movement out to others in incarnational mission.

Travelling Light, Dwelling Deep: a rhythm of life

Those who choose to travel some way with Contemplative Fire and support its ministry and outreach are called Companions on the Way, pioneers and pilgrims discerning the Way of Christ in a fractured world. Companions are invited to adopt a simple rhythm of life that draws on the tradition of church – particularly monastic communities – as well as the turning of the seasons and the passage of time and life.

Seeking to reclaim the treasure of these ancient patterns for everyday living, the Contemplative Fire rhythm of life is embodied in a trefoil, shaped by the graphic spirituality of its Celtic Christian inheritance. This trinitarian form reflects the three-fold dynamic of prayer, study and action; of being, knowing and doing. With the injunction to 'travel light and dwell deep', the challenge is expressed in terms that are accessible to believers and seekers alike, enabling both inreach and outreach.

Both for personal journeys and in community life, the Contemplative Fire trefoil encourages balanced and centred living, deeply grounded in the presence of the Holy. The leaves of the trefoil, *Still Waters*, *A Learning Journey* and *Across the Threshold*, each have their own quality and are equally weighted. In the middle is the place of unknowing and wordlessness, the whole trefoil held together in Trinitarian mystery.

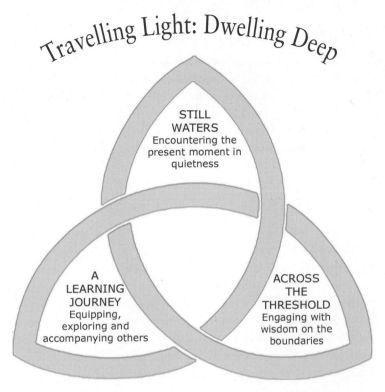

© Philip D Roderick 2001

Journey is also reflected in the dynamic of the trefoil. Just as the Chartres labyrinth has inspired pilgrims walking its intricate pattern, so the Contemplative Fire trefoil can become a two-dimensional space into which one can enter. During a Contemplative Fire community retreat on the Welsh coast, a huge trefoil, drawn out in the sand on the beach, provided a reflective path along which to walk. True to its Celtic roots, the path with no beginning and no end connects, flows and interweaves, resonating with each of the different persons of the Trinity. Thresholds are encountered in the crossing from one area to another, or in the stepping out from or into the interior. In such a space, deep journeying may be made, and transformation in Christ embraced.

Still Waters: encountering the present moment in quietness

Rooted in Scripture and the wisdom of the contemplative tradition, Still Waters is the call into stillness, silence and prayer as an integral part of a daily rhythm of life. In this invitation, Contemplative Fire seeks to be attentive to the intricacies of nature and the essence and energy of God as the Source, the Father.

Drawing on the silent practice of the rich monastic, Celtic and eremitical traditions, in small groups and in solitude, in the gentle movement of body prayer and in stillness, Contemplative Fire provides opportunities for the exploration and nurture of the sacrament of the present moment. The centred person of Christ, in his practice and teaching of withdrawal and prayer, inspires and enables patterns of busyness and distraction to be noticed, interrupted and transformed in a simple and regular discipline. Times of stillness, in the home, the workplace, in and out of doors, encourage the attitude of wonder and delight. Awareness of the breath and the body as a place of encounter with the creative energy of God brings the mind into the heart, strengthening the soul for the work of Love.

Within this rhythm, engagement with creation, which Celtic spirituality names as 'God's big book', is integral to the practice of being. Attentiveness to the placing of one's feet and connectedness with the earth, to colours, textures, shapes and fragrance, to the touch of the plants and earth, to the quality of the air, the movement of the sky and the feel of the wind, to the seasons of birth, growth, decay and death, all enable internal spaciousness and receptivity to the wisdom and love of God. In Contemplative Fire small groups and in the context of Quiet Gardens, urban oases, coastland and countryside, quietude becomes accessible to those hungry for space and the recovery of meaning. Whether words have failed in despair, are absent in loneliness, or have become overwhelming, this praxis becomes a doorway into the mystery of the Word and an invitation to become part of the eternal song of the universe.

This is not about escapism, or about catching one's breath before returning to the treadmill. Encounter with God in stillness is transforming in body, mind and spirit, enabling spaciousness in thought, attentiveness in the midst of busyness, detachment from distraction, and authenticity in compassion. The intention is not to shut out, to ignore or escape, but to be transfigured by the grace of God and energized by the generative love of the Trinity, from which flows a radical and contemplative discipleship.

A Learning Journey: equipping, exploring and accompanying others

The contemplative tradition speaks deeply and prophetically into our Western culture. When knowledge and success is prized and rewarded, where is the place for questions, failure and unknowing? When the longing is for certainty and progress, what do the qualities of stability, detachment and centredness have to teach us? Where is wisdom to be found in the search for meaning?

A Learning Journey focuses upon the seminal model and inspiration of Jesus and his equipping of the twelve. It is an invitation into a two-fold learning journey: looking out to and exploring the tradition, as well as learning to look within. In this rhythm we engage with the insights of the saints and mystics and honour the wisdom received through life experience, in ourselves and in one another. We encourage an open and enquiring engagement with the deep truths of the incarnation and with the ministry, teaching, death, resurrection and ascension of Jesus Christ. This is complemented by what may be described as learning from the 'felt-sense' of the sacramental nature of matter, both in creation and in the human body.

Reflective reading with discussion, listening and silence, the sharing of insight in threes, sevens and in open circles, praying in the body and awareness walking, are all opportunities for theological engagement and for the appreciation of questions rather than the simple provision of answers. Whether it is in theological reflection, in being heard by another through spiritual direction, or in the practice of *lectio divina*, a growing consciousness of being known by God is released. We begin to hear and know one another and ourselves as authentic people of presence and hope; this is a journey where human experience, our own and that inherited from the tradition and held within Scripture, becomes a threshold for receiving the mind of Christ.

Across the Threshold: engaging with wisdom on the boundaries

'If we live by the spirit, let us be guided by the Spirit' (Gal. 5.25). Across the Threshold: engaging with wisdom on the boundaries, represents the Holy Spirit, the comforter and challenger, the inspirer and often the outrageous guide. Discerning which boundary we are to walk, and sensing when and how to listen and respond to wisdom's surprising presence in the most unexpected places and people – this is a gift of the Holy Spirit.

In common with the mission of the whole Church, Contemplative Fire's rhythm of life holds within it the invitation and challenge of the Holy Spirit to live and witness with humility in places of the ordinary. At work, in studies, in the home and in the local community, companions seek to live in the way of Christ with an attitude of being present and open to the other. In doing so, we are drawn out of our comfort zone towards the edge. By grace our eyes and ears are attentive and softened and, increasingly, we find ourselves led through to genuine mutuality and open-heartedness. Be it in justice or compassion, in a readiness to reach out or to reach in, the Spirit illumines and instructs, dismantles barriers and builds bridges.

Nurtured by contemplative practice, silence and solitude become precursors to service. Within this rhythm of life, a dynamic emerges, where awareness of the now of God and our place within that presence enables a deeper engagement with the other. From within this energy, we are drawn to cross the thresholds of culture and experience in order to encounter and proclaim Christ in a new paradigm. We become hospitable and welcoming to wisdom revealed in others, better equipped to live Christ and to be the metaphor, 'contemplative fire'!

Sweet-Water Well

Helpful in clarifying how Contemplative Fire makes response to the creative tension between orthodoxy and exploration, between given kerygma and its integral dynamic of emergence, is the story of the two farmers, one Australian, one American. The latter complains he has so many cattle and so many acres that he has to spend thousands of dollars on barbed wire fencing to keep in the animals. The Australian farmer responds quietly by remarking that his property is so vast and his cattle so numerous, that the only way he can survive is for him to provide and sustain a sweet-water well at the heart of the land. The animals have the freedom to wander, but they rarely stray too far because they find themselves, time and again, drawn back to the sweet-water well.

Drinking from the sweet-water well of contemplative Christian theology offers a viable alternative to the all-too pervasive absolutism and lack of spaciousness that characterize much religious, political and cultural expression. In our experience, many who have left mainstream churches, or who have avoided going in, are often wounded and/or saddened by the competing snares of rigorism and literalism on the one hand and dogmatic liberalism in its more dismissive guise on the other. Such excesses of faith have proved to be deeply counter-productive for nurture in Christ. What is less than absolute all too often finds itself elevated into an absolute – be it biblical inerrancy, ritual niceties or the primacy of intellect over soul, of rationalism over mystery. The end result has been spiritual abuse in so many forms.

What can be done in response to this wounding? To recognize the pattern, interrupt the pattern and transform the pattern. This 'pattern interrupt', exemplified by Jesus and by the long line of saints, provides the agenda for Contemplative Fire's pedagogy of wholeness and holiness, and it underpins our enthusiasm for education and spiritual formation rooted and grounded in the love of God.

Call, Equip, Send

Strongly felt and discerned from the very inception of Contemplative Fire has been our response to God's calling, equipping and sending. We have received God's prompting from without and God's confirmation from within, and so actively respond to the call to the Way of Christ. The challenge to equip and to accompany others in their discipleship fuels Contemplative Fire's emphasis on appreciative inquiry and spiritual formation. The invitation, of course, is to more than self-development and community building. Contemplative Fire, celebrating the 'essence and energy' of God, knows itself to be moved as much by the injunction to communicate and to serve as by the vocation to interiority.

Contemplative Fire has come into being, at least in part, for those on or over the edge of the institutional and mainstream churches. For some, Contemplative Fire is their 'church'; others choose to have a both/and path. Within this membership, there is a significant continuum of personality types and spiritual profiles, ranging from hermit to hyper-activist! The hyphens embedded within the seminal phrase 'contemplation-in-action' indicate a rich admixture of character and gift, of orientation and expression. Mutual respect and encouragement, despite difference of emphasis and charism, are key norms within this emergent community. Understanding these differences within individuals is a necessary ingredient in 'sending' and supporting Companions on the Way. This missiology is deeply rooted in our shared experience as 'partakers of the divine nature' (2 Peter 1.4).

How is this injunction to call, equip and send given body and texture within Contemplative Fire? It happens primarily through a series of small and large group events, and in an exploration of proven and often ancient spiritual practices. Undergirding this contemplative-apostolic focus is the knowledge that deep structure can give rise to creativity and playfulness; that the discipline of order can foster spontaneity and freedom. In so far as the tradition of the Church is approached with openness and integrity, so the interior dynamic of that tradition is given space and sustenance to flower in the lives of individuals and groups.

Regionally Dispersed

As a network community, Contemplative Fire makes provision for some large events – Gatherings, Pilgrimages to Now/here and training series – which highlight the necessary convergence in Christ of the journey inward and the journey outward.

Gatherings

How does Contemplative Fire worship and present liturgy? As a new region of Contemplative Fire begins to seed and take root, with the blessing of area bishop and local clergy, early to emerge is a regular Gathering. Wherever possible these will be centred on the Eucharist, celebrating God's presence in sacrament and liturgy, in art, music, body prayer and procession, in anointing and healing and in shared silence. Drawing inspiration from the lectionary readings for the day and from the ancient pattern of the liturgy of Eastern and Western churches, a local planning group engages in a creative and prayerful *lectio divina* process with the scriptural texts and the liturgical season to design the Gathering.

Our Gatherings could happen anywhere. They have unfolded in a variety of places: from the nooks, crannies and prayerful spaces of a seventh-century abbey, to a school hall; from a restored seventeenth-century barn, to a beach, or a little-used monastic chapel. In autumn and winter, services are often held by candlelight, and outdoors where possible in the summer. Within the pattern of the liturgy we engage with the Church's themes and seasons, texts and teachings, in 'low-tech' and thought-provoking ways. In our worship, artists and musicians share their compositions; CDs of contemporary jazz give way to early medieval chant; body prayer is balanced with profound stillness.

Pilgrimage to Now/here

A celebration of the natural world, be it parkland or seashore, woodland or mountainside, is a core ingredient of the Contemplative Fire 'mix'. The pilgrimage to now/here draws upon the earliest tradition of pilgrimage that honours not so much the destination but the journey itself. Contemplative Fire leaders in different areas find warm and welcoming, naturally congenial contexts in which to gather people for some input at the end of, or midway through, the day.

Locally Earthed

On a smaller scale of nurture and belonging, we are seeing develop a number of small group processes. Within the frame of holistic learning, each group has two co-facilitators equipped by Contemplative Fire, together with a fluid and yet formed structure for challenge and support. Groups generally meet in each other's homes to share food, wine, silence and stories.

Open Circles

These are occasions for engaging the mind and heart in shared stillness, mystical theology and Scripture, in order to discern wisdom. The ideal number for Open Circles is anything from six to twelve, meeting monthly on average. Perhaps a book from the contemplative Christian tradition is chosen and worked through gradually; members may take it in turn to lead a session, month by month, in presenting some reflection meaningful for them and pertinent to those on or exploring the Way of Christ. Integral to the Open Circle dynamic is openness both to newcomers and to honest responses to faith and life, together with the sharing of high calibre resources and periodic stillness.

Threes

Integrated in the pattern of the rhythm of life is an understanding of the learning journey as accompanied and mutual, where wisdom and the holy are encountered both within and in the other. 'Threes' provides a form where three people meet regularly for a structured two-hour session of deep listening. The process allows time for each person to speak their story in complete confidence, without debate or discussion, woven through with silence. Often common themes emerge out of the silences, surprising connections are made and wisdom revealed. We learn not only to listen with respect to the other, but also to ourselves, without fear of condemnation or the need for explanation. Dilemmas and struggles are named; hopes and dreams are articulated. Silence gives spaciousness and time in which to wonder. This is holy ground.

Sevens: Way beyond Religion

This is a regular meeting of about seven people in which to celebrate the major festivals of the Christian year with food for the body and soul, and with deep sharing and blessing. The process is centred around a meal – breakfast, lunch or supper. Using simple evocative liturgies that draw on the Christian contemplative tradition, each meeting begins with prayer and worship, moving into an agape style meal with open conversation. Following the meal, reflective catalysts are provided – literary, visual or textual, and insights shared. During the closing liturgy, time in silence is given for waiting upon God to discern what might be the invitation or challenge received during the session. The liturgy closes with prayer for one another and for the world.

Still Waters Groups

These sessions provide opportunities for inreach and outreach through shared silence. Local groups meet in homes or in community spaces for the refreshment of stillness and movement, enabling a deepening of personal contemplative practice and gentle accepting companionship with others. Centred upon Christ, drawing on Scripture or the writings from the mystical tradition, with a simple visual focus, such as a candle or icon, Still Waters provides spaciousness and time in which to rest in God.

Validating different gifts

With Jesus, the twelve and the first Christian community providing the primary model for Contemplative Fire, it is instructive to note from biblical texts that all followers of Christ were to be participants in the life of the Holy Spirit. As Paul indicates in Romans 12.6–8: 'We have gifts that differ according to the grace given to us.' The apostle identifies prophecy, ministry, teaching, exhortation, giving, leading and being compassionate. Then 1 Corinthians 12.4–11 and 27–31 outline how spiritual gifts, often with a very practical orientation and application, were apportioned throughout the community of believers.

Crucial to the seeding and flourishing of local groups and regions within the dispersed network of Contemplative Fire, is the gradual nurturance of every member in the process of stepping into his or her own authority in God. Authentic and effective discipleship and responsibility then flow. In consequence, the significance and particular gifts and callings within the body of Christ become apparent. The challenge is always to discern the most appropriate, sensitive and yet robust ways in which to affirm both the priesthood of all believers and the variety of gifts within that collective, and, at the same time, the particular charism and order of bishop, priest and deacon.

The capacity to draw out the finest in each person needs to be in evidence as one of the key attributes of educators, spiritual directors, counsellors and clergy. Ingredients core to the recruitment and development of leaders and facilitators of small and large groups include: a pastoral heart, a deep and inquiring Christ-centred spiritual practice, a lively knowledge and love of the Scriptures, and of the golden thread of the embodied faith of the saints and mystics of the Church. Priests and pilgrims, prophets and poets, scientists and artists, parents and children – all are made one in the lived mystery of the risen Christ.

'Bless what there is for being'[1]

Contemplative Fire, in its rhythm of life rooted in the Trinity, and in its commitment to the nurturance of pilgrims and leaders in the Way of Christ, is only at a beginning. This is a path of knowing and unknowing, one that is raising questions for us about the unfathomable nature of God and of how to be church. As a community, we are both challenged and inspired by our inheritance of faith, and believe that our calling to 'create a community of Christ at the edge' requires a re-imagining and re-presenting of the dynamic of tradition. Within a context of woundedness, our desire is to be enfolded in the life of the Spirit; for forgiveness, healing, reconciliation and openness to thrive in all of creation. We remain fragile, emergent and Christ centred. We are called into a depth of delight and a gifting of presence that, we hope and pray, is enabling the love of God to flourish as a sweet water well in a new landscape.

Contact information

Contemplative Fire:
www.contemplativefire.org
info@contemplativefire.org

The Quiet Garden Movement:
www.quietgarden.co.uk
quiet.garden@ukonline.co.uk

Note

1 Taken from W. H. Auden, 'Precious Five'.

13

Mission @ The Crossing:
Where Real Church Meets Real Life

STEPHANIE SPELLERS, CHRISTOPHER
ASHLEY, MARIE HARKEY AND
KIRSTEN WESSELHOEFT

Kirsten's Story. . .

For most of my life, church has been a place where people multi-tasked. At my grandparents' church in Ohio, I could look down the pew and see my great-uncle balancing his checkbook, my mother filling in the picture on the front of the bulletin, maybe even someone nodding off in the corner. My grandfather, though, was the most brazen: under the guise of 'keeping the children quiet,' he would draw on the backs of my cousins' and my hands—the margins of the bulletin being apparently insufficient to occupy him for what must have been hour-long sermons. My grandfather could draw two things well—bunny rabbits and dogwood flowers—and that is what he drew. Every time we visited, we would solemnly follow him out of church, our lavishly-adorned hands folded behind our backs, for even then we understood that this was not an appropriate church activity. Then again, when it came right down to it, Grandpa was not behaving much differently from anyone else in that church.

I look back now and smile at those Sundays. The bunny rabbits and dogwood flowers are some of the strongest memories

I have of a grandfather I lost too soon. But there is a slight bittersweetness to the memory. My grandfather, one of the most spiritual and Christ-loving people I have known, encountered God in countless places in his life. Church, it is sad to say, was probably not first among them.

It took me more than a year of being a member of The Crossing community to realize that it had never once occurred to me to pull out a pen and draw flowers in the margins of my worship sheet. Because my whole self was being wholly engaged in worship and community, I did not have the time or the brain space or the distracted urge to multi-task. For me this was the freshest kind of church experience—a kind of worship where I was being asked to respond and participate and to be, in that moment and that place, in relationship with God and fellow followers of Christ.

I like to think that if my grandfather were alive today, and if I could bring him to The Crossing, you would not see dogwood flowers on anyone's hand.

The Crossing: where real church meets real life

Kirsten's experience is common for young adults, especially the ones who make their way to The Crossing. Whether they grew up in church or not, many have reluctantly concluded that Christian faith is more a social or cultural accessory than a way of life that makes a difference. For emerging generations who demand authenticity and crave commitments that matter, church is not worth the trouble if it is merely a building where people sit in private contemplation or scribble on their bulletins, passive observers obliged to witness but take no active role in the work enacted by holy hands in the distance.

What kind of church *would* be worth the trouble? One that compels us to follow Jesus with all that we are: body, mind, heart and soul. One that draws on the beauty, weight and wisdom of tradition, and sets those traditions in a mutually transformative relationship with the life and culture in which we are imbedded. We have heard and grown weary of the simplistic binaries: high church vs. low church, progressive vs. evangelical, traditional vs. contemporary, sacred vs. secular. Like faithful Anglicans before us, we seek a both/and path. We seek to become a community of Jesus' followers at once rooted in local context and in sacramental traditions. Planted in deep, rich soil, we are convinced that we will hear more of God and participate more fully in God's life and mission.

This dual hope has shaped our community from its inception. Our priest and lead organizer, the Reverend Stephanie Spellers, began working at St Paul's Episcopal Cathedral in Boston in June 2005 (a day after her ordination). As part of her Cathedral duties, she was tasked with starting a new young adult worship service. Instead of launching a new service, she began setting up one-to-one meetings with young adults in the Cathedral congregation and in the surrounding community. Eventually, she drew together a team of nine people in their twenties, thirties, and early forties who committed to meet every other week to pray, listen to each others' passions and hopes, and imagine a new way of being in Christian community. That initial group included artists, musicians, activists, Buddhists, a yoga teacher, high-church liturgists, evangelicals and gospel lovers, some Episcopalians, some non-Episcopalians and an agnostic. Different as we were, we shared a passion for people who knew little of church, had been turned out of church, or were present but holding back in church (and we represented all three groups). We had a heart for people of any age who might be yearning for a life-changing encounter with God and community, and hoping to be part of God's work of reconciliation and wholeness within and beyond the church.

For five months, that initial crew gathered around take-out Indian food in a funky basement office a few miles from our host church. In that open space, we shared the varied spiritual practices that linked us most closely to God. And we prayed around an open question: what kind of Christian community would welcome and engage our neighbors and fellow seekers who want little to do with church? What could we share from the ancient treasure trove, and what experiences far from church would we now claim as holy? By the end of our discernment period, we agreed we would head into the Cathedral and create a new worship community, one that fused Anglican and sacramental traditions with the pulse, color and hope we experience in urban life.

Since the spring of 2006, when we opened the Cathedral doors for our first Thursday night worship gathering, we have kept this bicultural commitment to local context and traditions. It's a bit like the approach of the R&B artists whose grooves we bring to the altar: they know the old forms well enough to play with them, riff on them, groove on them, in order to open hearts and express the soul that's been there all along. We seek to live that ancient/future fusion in all parts of our common life, especially in these seven areas: collaborative leadership, wider church relationships, rule for real life, justice and service, formation and small groups, the Eucharist and music.

Collaborative Leadership

There is a priest at The Crossing. "Rev. Steph" wears a collar and a stole as she celebrates the Eucharist every week. But from the beginning, we have understood her role as that of facilitator and animator. She is not the sole dispenser of the Good News, nor do her ideas about organizing our common life trump everyone else's. Her role is to take all the resources at her disposal—education, formation, experience, sacramental function, authority as one set apart by ordination—and use them to activate people's recognition of their own authority as leaders doing God's work in the church and in the world.

While we have not tried to create a leaderless organization, we have fostered a collaborative leadership structure that trusts the gifts and voices of the people. It helps to think of leadership in this mode as a web rather than a ladder. Ideas flow around the circle, rarely from the top down, and all the leaders are encouraged to look around at each other for partnership and accountability, rather than up to the priest. This commitment means we listen deeply to each other and to the community. And it is hard work.

The critical test for our commitment to collaborative leadership came early in our life together. The question was: who will preach? From the first gathering to this day, lay people have done almost all of the preaching at The Crossing. But it is by no means a free-for-all. One leader takes responsibility for a month's preaching at a time, getting more comfortable and insightful with each week. Our sermons are actually five-minute reflections grounded in scripture, traditions, reason, the leader's story and the wider community's story. The leader receives guidelines for doing reflections, and then partners actively with Rev. Steph and one other community member throughout the month. Immediately after the reflection, during worship, there is a brief talk-back time for some people in the gathered body to respond for one minute each with their own stories or insights. This is a far cry from the priest sitting alone in her study writing a sermon, delivering it on a Sunday and moving straight to the Nicene Creed. In this incarnation, people throughout the community learn to trust lay people's voices—and thus their own—as wise and powerful messengers of the gospel.

We have found that practicing leadership in this way requires more time, more energy and a willingness on the part of the priest and other leaders to let go of ego and help others to shine with the light of Christ. Why on earth would we choose this model? Because we believe participating in God's realm here on earth requires recognizing and encouraging what God is doing in each person, especially the ones who have historically been silenced or disempowered by the Church. Because we all need to practice letting go of agendas and outcomes, and instead to be genuinely open to the gifts others bring—whether it is the homeless man who prays beautifully and at great length, or the attorney who heads the Massachusetts Bar Association. Because we believe the most important question to answer is, 'What can we do together for God?' And everyone should have an answer to that question.

Wider-Church Relationships

When you are based in a Cathedral, there is no pretending you are a free agent without a wider church family. Instead of apologizing for being part of a denominational body, we take this unique opportunity to subvert people's assumptions about church, even as we attempt to recast the institution from the inside.

Our funding comes from a combination of sources, including pledges and giving from our own members, foundation grants, diocesan support and finally support from the Cathedral. Our priest began as a paid member of the Cathedral staff, but that is no longer the case. Nevertheless, we identify as a congregation that is within the larger Cathedral fold. That means we accept the calling to serve the Diocese of Massachusetts and The Episcopal Church, welcoming pilgrims from other congregations that are testing the emergent waters, traveling to share resources and principles that have guided our development, connecting with other pioneering ministries that are teaching us new ways of being God's people in the world. Last year, we also partnered with the Episcopal Clergy Association in Massachusetts to co-host an Emergent Learning Day with author and speaker Phyllis Tickle. We may be on the frontier, and we may be cobbling resources to pay our way like many other church-plants, but that is no reason to be Lone Rangers.

That said, our goal is not, in one member's words, to perform a bait and switch, luring people into a static institution that will not welcome their gifts, voices or presence. So we welcome new pilgrims to join us in the revolution, to bring their passion to the project of loving and changing the Church, even as we join Jesus in loving and changing the world. When we effect the right balance, tradition and context—church and world—are ever transforming one another.

Rule for Real Life

In the spring of 2008, our community reached a critical stage in its development: people wanted to be official members. Our leaders looked at each other and wondered, 'What should we do now?' The conventional wisdom about young adults is that they do not want to join things, to tie themselves to institutions. But we have learned in our community that people of all ages are hungry for commitment. When we commit to relationships, romantic or otherwise, they give shape and meaning and priorities to our hyper-networked lives. A life without commitment or discipline is not very satisfying for long.

As we asked how to make membership tangible and meaningful, how to create an accountable community of Christians sharing a journey, we opted to craft a community rule of life. A Christian rule is a commitment to a life shaped like Jesus' by particular actions, what Eugene Peterson (following Nietzsche) calls 'a long obedience in the same direction.'[1] The point is not simply to name values, but to make the same choices, over and over again, until they make us more like Jesus and our community more like his.

As we meditated together on the traditional monastic vows of poverty, chastity and obedience in light of our ordinary lives, we identified a small but rigorous set of commitments: radical welcome, justice and service, spiritual practice, stewardship of money and resources, relational integrity, and worship in community.[2] And we created structures to support members who journey with those promises. To define our membership by these commitments opens it to all those who are part of our common life, even those who cannot physically join us on Thursdays or those who maintain membership in a parish church. They only need to share our hunger to follow Jesus in a Way that has a particular shape, and our desire to walk faithfully in the company of this particular community of pilgrims.

The great English pastoral theologian Martin Thornton has called a rule of life one of the essential elements of Christian proficiency. In the same way, we find having a rule is a sign of and spur to our emerging maturity as a community of serious disciples.

Justice and Service

At the close of worship, we are dismissed to 'go in peace to love and serve the Lord.' There is a powerful connection between experiencing God in worship and prayer, and then participating in God's work of justice, love and reconciliation. For us, worshiping an incarnate God means loving God's creations in all their physicality, and recognizing the sacred not just in all life, but in all *of* life.

Our local context makes that mission urgent and lends it concrete form. At The Crossing, we have taken the Church's call to healing and reconciliation and used it to shape our own community's identity. By practicing reconciliation as a body, we get practice with the work of 'mov[ing] out to join God in healing, freeing, and blessing all people' (these words close our mission statement). This internal reconciliation manifests in part through our practice of radical welcome, especially with lesbian, gay, bisexual and transgendered people who continue to be on the margins both of the Church and the world of which we are a part. We have not stopped at being a 'welcoming and affirming' church, but work to be a church that actively stands with LGBT people on the margins. This commitment is a constantly present reminder, to those inside and outside our community, of our commitment to radical love and relational justice.

When we turn outward—whether sending representatives to partner with churches in Kenya, serving regularly with partners in nearby homeless ministries, or consciously developing a new justice and outreach ministry that facilitates our engagement in collective social action and service—we do not envision ourselves as a healed and pure church going to save a sick, broken and impure world. Rather, we hope to bless and heal both our church and our secular world. Again, we strive not to see a binary: both of these spheres need God's grace with equal urgency, and we are fully part of them both.

Formation and Small Groups

Before worship one Thursday evening, a group is discussing Richard Hooker and Anglican theology in a small group titled 'Episcopal Church 101.' After worship on the same night, students from nearby Emerson College come to take part in a forum on sexuality and faith. This is formation at The Crossing, helping people to understand and claim our traditions even as we bring faith to bear on the most urgent questions in our context.

Forming disciples is one of the most ancient mandates of the Church. From the beginning, small groups of Jesus' followers gathered in homes to 'continue in the apostles' teachings and the prayers.' Small groups are one of the most important places for discipleship formation in a context like ours. Our Minister for Community Life and other leaders have been trained in the principles of community organizing in order to listen deeply to people's longings and big questions. Then they facilitate the formation of small groups designed to help people at various stages to live out our faith and follow the Way of Jesus in every area of our lives.

How does this look in action? In a six-month period, members organized a catechesis class (Episcopal Church 101), a three-part forum on faith and sexuality, ongoing covenant groups based on our Rule for Real Life, a book study on prayer, a bible study in a local bar, a centering prayer group, and a regular prayer service in the park across from the church in the summertime. A group also launched Urban Adventures to explore our Boston context and build relationships with each other. In each instance, we acknowledged the importance of small groups and formation to every vital Christian community. But the shape, times, content and leadership? Those must be formed by context.

Eucharist

From the beginning, our leaders were passionate about reclaiming ancient spiritual practices and placing them at the center of our life, week after week. But we also knew we would need to translate those practices so that they would be accessible and yet powerful, mysterious and yet perceptibly transformative. Nowhere was this more important than in the Eucharist.

We were not always sure that The Crossing would be a eucharistic community. If the communion table were front and center, some believed it would be too difficult to welcome people who had been wounded by church or who came with little or no background. As we shared our stories, we came to surprising consensus: the presence of Jesus, made known in this sacrament, makes us who we are. Despite our great differences, we could not imagine being a Christian community, or welcoming others to be pilgrims on the Way, without meeting Jesus in the breaking of bread. The question became, how could we tell and live that story, the Jesus story, in ways that would neither alienate nor over-explain, but instead open the way to a mystery and new life?

Some of the resulting practices are novel: the prayers of the people immediately precede the eucharistic prayer, which means the liturgy of the table (including our priest's extemporaneous eucharistic prayer) quite literally flows out of the prayers of all the people. All the people are invited to lift their hands during the eucharistic celebration and to extend them toward the table at the blessing of the elements. It is apparent that we are building and expressing our community's relational character, our constant search for Jesus in one another. As sacramental theology, this is unremarkable. Even as liturgical practice, it is by no means unprecedented. Yet members have said worship like this teaches us anew what God is doing at every communion table. 'Behold the Lamb of God,' says the Rite I liturgy after the prayer of humble access; many of us have learned in this community how to actually look around, at that moment, and see Jesus.

We lean only lightly on the prayer book's set language, at least in our visible practice, yet those who are familiar with the liturgy and with eucharistic prayer construction will detect the skeleton of the ancient order. This is by design. The prayer book often becomes a sort of exoskeleton: it makes our shape and structure visible, but sometimes hides the living community of God's people, the many cultures that shape that community, the language and prayers that are at the heart of the community. Instead, we imagine that the liturgy is our endoskeleton, hidden but powerfully present. It is essential to work with and to translate the traditional forms, to show the world our Anglican bone structure. But it is just as important to show our community's face, and in so doing, to show the faces of the living Christ.

Music

There is little that is more faithful to Anglican tradition than doing liturgy in the vernacular. Our first commitment is to common prayer, and this means more than prayer that is common the world over (something of a holdover from the days of empire, when colonials could expect to travel from Lancashire to Lagos and experience the same liturgy). Common prayer is also prayer in the language that is common to the people on the ground. The highest compliment we can pay to our traditions is to give them life in this day, so that the Good News is accessible and compelling to the real people around us.

More than almost anything else, music is where people listen for their 'language' in worship. If we hear the music of our hearts, the music of our home cultures, then we have some clue as to whether we are genuinely welcome. As any veteran of multicultural ministry or the 1990s' 'worship wars' can attest, music sets certain boundaries, not least around race and age. In our commitment to radical welcome, we had to discern a musical language that would announce welcome and value to the groups with whom we sought to be in relationship.

In particular, given our location in downtown Boston and our young adult leadership, we had to pay attention to 'the groove.' Music rooted in the grooves of popular music—much of it influenced by African-American culture—has a powerful impact on people of all races and ages, all nations and tongues. It lives in our cars, in our kitchens, in our iPods, as well as in our memories of tough and happy times. It moves us and can certainly move us toward God.

In the same way, we found that the great hymns, chants and prayers of the Church continue to speak to our world and our hearts today, shaping our faith as surely as any formation class might. At one time, our Music Director was a Pentecostal young woman with little experience of the Episcopal musical tradition. She was practically ecstatic about working with these 'new' hymns and chants, thrilled about the range of ways to speak of the trinitarian God, God's mission and our relationship with God and with one another. There was no reason to throw out this baby with the bathwater. We only needed to run some fresh water.

Out of those two insights, contextual and traditional, grew a fresh musical style. We sing many of the great hymns, known to some of us from childhood, reaching others for the first time. But we sing them over grooves, fitting their melodies to a sense of rhythm and movement that celebrates our bodies and blesses the bump and thump that animates life just outside our church's doors. Does 'Come Thou Fount of Every Blessing' need further tweaking to suit its Appalachian home? Perhaps not. But for Tremont Street on Boston Common, the song's joyous shout rings truer with a syncopated skip in its step. And as all kinds of people walk off the street and join their voices to ours, many find themselves not only right at home, but full of the Holy Spirit.

*   *   *

Concluding Thoughts

Early in our life together, leaders at The Crossing were hunting for shorthand to describe the amalgam emerging in our midst. We decided on 'The Crossing: where real church meets real life.' These simple words were meant as a signal to our neighbors and a reminder to our leaders. First, this church would not shy away from boldly reclaiming the things of 'real church': Eucharist, priests, set prayers, sacramental traditions, spiritual disciplines, a lively and life-changing relationship with Jesus Christ. Just as significantly, this church would embody authentic community that was not afraid of 'real life' with its big questions, messy edges, heartfelt grooves, incredible beauty and gaping, God-shaped holes. That dual calling still anchors us. And it demands that we announce the countercultural truth of the gospel so that God's love can penetrate deep into the heart of real urban life, crossing boundaries and bridging chasms until we all find our way home to the God who has been there all along.

Notes

1 Eugene Peterson, 2000, *A Long Obedience in the Same Direction: Discipleship in an Instant Society*, Downers Grove, Ill.: Intervarsity Press.

2 See The Crossing's 'Rule for Real Life' at http://www.thecrossingboston.org.

3 Martin Thornton, 1988, *Christian Proficiency*, Cambridge, Mass.: Cowley Publications. See Chapter 5 on Christian rule.

14

Blesséd: A Sacramental Perspective of Alternative Worship with Young People

SIMON RUNDELL

A small child returned from Mass and asked his mother, 'Mummy, God is here with us isn't he?' 'Oh yes,' his mother replied. 'And he is here, in this kitchen, isn't he?' 'Yes, yes he is ....' 'And he's here, at this kitchen table?' 'Err, yes ...' his mother replied rather more cautiously. 'And he's here, in this sugar bowl then, isn't he?' 'Well, err ... yes, I suppose so ....' Quick as a flash, the lad grabs the bowl and pops his hand on top: 'Got 'im!'

How we would love to be able to capture God, to contain him in our sugar bowls, or trap him between the pages of a book, or keep our notion of God frozen in the aspic of that which we regard as tradition. But God is beyond all that: to think that God can be fully captured by Scripture or by any other concrete construction would be to bring him down to a very small level indeed (De Lubac, 1960, pp. 2–13).

The sacraments have never sought to capture God, but merely to reflect some of his essence. The Greek word used for sacrament is *mysterion* from which we get the English word mystery. In seeking God in worship, in seeking the unknowable, the mysterious, we turn to signs and symbols. In the language of postmodernism, this is semiotics.

Postmodernism suggested that our cosy prejudices were subjective (Ward, 2003, p. 170). Even if young people didn't know the language of postmodernism and got confused between Jacques Derrida and Jacques Cousteau, they clearly now sense that authority is defunct and sources of truth are suspect: the Internet can provide you with a million different interpretations and all or none of them may be true.

Alternative worship began as a rejection of traditional church and traditional worship and rode the wave of postmodern thought. As it continues to seek to be radical, it discovers that a priori concepts of worship have to be dismantled and new ways of worship need to be explored. In the same way that postmodern thought has become eclectic, so postmodern worship has embraced a wide variety of style and spirituality without concern for where it has come from. Alternative worship defies traditional labels of churchmanship. The result has been the rediscovery of ritual and a greater emphasis on sign and symbol as a mechanism for reaching out towards God.

The natural territory of signs and wonders, of sacrament and ritual, is the catholic tradition. We must be careful not to misunderstand 'Catholic' with a capital 'C' and 'catholic' with a lower-case 'c'. The former usually refers to the Roman Catholic Church whilst the catholic tradition is more a style and a theology than a denomination. 'Catholic' itself means universal, as in the stated belief in the 'one holy, catholic and apostolic church' that is a feature of the Nicene Creed. Within the catholic tradition there exist many church affiliations and so in this way it is more appropriate to a postmodern understanding that rejects a single point of reference or authority.

Being catholic is not just about incense and candles (staple tools of alternative worship), it is more than Gregorian chant and any of the other affectations of faux catholicism; it is about a fundamental way of looking at the incarnation and the world as affected by the incarnation: the unknowable can be made partially known and the sacraments can provide a mechanism to that encounter – we should not be concerned with the immediate but trust in the power of Christ to capture the spiritual yearning within most people, young and old.

The original multi-sensory worship was the liturgy celebrated in the Basilica of the eighth century: a place where sight, sound, smell and taste ensured that we sought to engage with God's wondrous creation and to try to express the inexpressible. By worshipping with more than just our lips and seeking faith without necessarily seeking understanding, we celebrate our humanity as glorified by the incarnation (Anselm, *Prosologium*) in all its diversity (Psalm 150.6). The Mass we celebrate today is not the Mass of Hippolytus, it is not the Mass of the eighth-century Basilica, it is not the Mass of Cranmer, nor is it the Tridentine Mass; it is a successor to all of them. It is the result of much borrowing, adapting and changing over time. Tradition is, above all, a dynamic entity, not a static museum piece.

Blesséd is a group which seeks to be unconventional, to remain true to its Anglo-Catholic heritage and yet embrace new ways of encountering God through sign and symbol and most especially through the sacraments.

Fundamentally, I believe that our primary encounter with God in worship is not an intellectual one, but an emotive one. Worship is one of the first ways that seekers of faith encounter Christ, and when asked about their first dip in the worship ocean, they do not reflect on worship in terms of reason or logic, of whether they were convinced by the argument, but in terms of how it made them feel. The mountaintop experience of the transfiguration came about by a wondrous encounter with the divine, not by intellectual engagement.

Blesséd sought, therefore, to replace the rather simplistic approach of evangelism to young people ('let me tell you a story about Jesus, kids …') with an emotional experience and a glimpse of the divine. Mark Yaconelli has written powerfully in his book *Contemplative Youth Ministry*, of the deep spirituality that is a key marker of young people, who yearn for a deep emotional experience with the other, and who are more open than most to a full-on encounter with God (Yaconelli, 2006). The sacramental direction of the group arose out of situation and context: a deeply Anglo-Catholic church[1] in urban Portsmouth began youth ministry to the unchurched, putting them into the sacred space almost by accident, lit a few candles and set the incense burning. Before we knew where we were, God got involved.

Clearly, originating in such a sacramental church, the sacramental life could not be avoided; surprisingly, though, it became a form of identification for the young people. On one occasion, when we were planning an act of worship, a number of our young people independently said, 'Well, it has to be a Mass, doesn't it?' They sought to define themselves in terms of their relationship to the sacrament and yet they were not constrained by the traditions of it.

As we explored the Mass, with young people on the inside and on the very edge of the church, with communicants, non-communicants and with the deeply hostile, a new understanding was revealed: each element of the Mass was seen as being up for grabs, fair game for a radical interpretation and a retelling of the story. It became a major part of the evangelization of these young people.

As Pete Ward discussed in his book *Mass Culture*, the Mass is truly an evangelistic opportunity and a missionary tool (Ward, 1999). It provides a unique opportunity for expressing the salvation story and the joy of the resurrection in word, song, action and ritual. The Mass provides both fixed points of reference and an ever-changing cycle of encounter with God, and this mix of the familiar and the challenging provides a framework on which to hang new explorations of worship; rather than being a limit to fresh expressions of worship, it forms a skeleton upon which a new creation is formed (2 Cor. 5.17).

Within Blesséd we have spoken unashamedly of the Mass because it is a classical English word, and although Roman Catholicism has in recent years hijacked it, it is the only word that describes effectively the whole service of word and sacrament joined together. 'Holy communion' refers only to a small part of the whole ritual, 'Eucharist' to a specific prayer within that ritual. It is a 'divine liturgy' in the Orthodox sense, an encounter with God through mechanisms which are not, and should not be, fully understood.

In order to facilitate this encounter, all have been welcome to participate and share in the sacrament. Within the Anglican tradition it is customary for the sacrament to be denied to those who have not undergone sacramental preparation and the administration of another of the nine sacraments: confirmation. However, God issues a welcome to all to encounter him; so at a Blesséd Mass, the blessed sacrament continues to be offered to any who come forward for it. It is a valid sacrament, and, in the understanding of many, is the real body and blood of Christ (for he said that himself, and who are we to deny what our Lord said of himself). Can any of us claim to fully understand these mysteries? Our philosophy is this: let us administer the sacrament freely and with grace, and let God sort out the rest.

Blesséd took something well loved and cherished and gave it a new slant. Nothing within the mass is there without purpose or significance, so a fresh, youth-orientated approach afforded new ways of communicating ancient truths. By maintaining the shape of the liturgy as described by Dom Gregory Dix (1945, p. 48) and at times radically reinterpreting it, the whole encounter with God is re-explored, and new nuances and themes develop: eucharistic prayers are mimed, creeds are given a rave feel in a language not spoken by anyone in the audience, the Gloria is tap-danced and the liturgy is shared by all as dough is kneaded, baked and broken across a single act of worship.

The end result is something that is at once both familiar and yet very challenging. The comfort found in ritual and repetition is transformed by new and risky ways of looking at them (Ward, 2004, pp. 37–51). The symbolism of a past age is brought crashing into a modern era as the gently tinkling bells of the eucharistic elevation are replaced by a guitarist's heavily distorted power chord.[2]

For a priest, this can be challenging. The groups planning the liturgy are sometimes treading a balance between the sacred and the profane; challenging imagery (such as a foetus wearing a crown, tattooed and pierced) and the most radical indie, metal or dance music are always pushing boundaries of taste, decency and the structures of the church. However innovatively expressed, these sacraments are always within the boundaries of canon law, even though Blesséd has never been a respecter of liturgical boundaries or the committees which police them!

Like many youth phenomena, the initial phase of Blesséd has passed, and the young people who came together for it have since moved on, to university, to work and at the same time to different expressions of church in which to encounter the sacred. And the moment it starts to appear stale it must, like the soap opera 'Brookside', or the cast of the first two series of 'Skins', be discarded and replaced with something new. Otherwise it will become like those Christian gatherings in Holiday Campsites that have moved from the radical to the established, losing its place at the cutting edge of faith.

This means that work with young people must be continually reinvented. In the past few years, the whole community of Blesséd has changed; this is both a boon and a challenge. There is a great temptation to reuse material from the dim and distant past because it will be unfamiliar to the new congregation, and yet their new insights and perspectives mean that the old is simply inappropriate. New forms of worship and expression are needed to capture the present group's vitality. Furthermore, young people are becoming increasingly technically proficient, and so they have seen all the old stuff on YouTube and know and love it well; it simply cannot be reused.[3]

So where does Blesséd go from here? Hopes and dreams to develop Blesséd as a proper non-Parochial Ecclesial Community have, frankly, foundered, and the challenges of maintaining a sense of true community with those who have no concept of physical community are immense. Blesséd utilizes all the modern forms of social networking, and this is effective to an extent, but it is in the sacramental encounter where the purpose of the group becomes clearest. So, if Blesséd isn't a formal, licensed, constituted or commissioned community, or an official brand of the Fresh Expressions movement, which it predates, what then will it look like in a few more years' time? It will, I sense, continue to be a roving resource and an irritant; an inspiration to some and a folly to others; a burner of carpets and good ideas, and a shot in the arm for any seeking to find a new place to encounter God in the Eucharist. And whilst there remain young people seeking more than the superficial or the banal, Blesséd will continue to work with, subvert and inspire them.

There is not a single model of youth evangelism that fits all groups of young people, and neither is there a single model of youth worship that is appropriate for all. The call to proclaim afresh for each generation the timeless truths of the gospel, and to provide glimpses of God through his most blessed sacraments – which are as ageless as the good news itself – has never been more pressing. Blesséd has shown that by drawing upon the sacramental heart of the faith, and yet placing it in a new context, and by challenging expected norms, it reflects the countercultural aspirations of many young people. For some who have encountered it, it has proved life changing and inspirational, for others it has been deeply offensive and challenging, and for the majority, it has been quaintly mystifying.

Mystery is good. Mystery is at the heart of the Godhead. Through this sacramentally focused youth ministry we are reminded that God cannot simply be kept in the sugar bowl.

References

Anselm, *Prosologium,* 'Faith seeking understanding', 1, viewed on 19 January 2009 at http://www.fordham.edu/halsall/basis/anselm-proslogium.html.

Gregory Dix, 1945, *The Shape of the Liturgy,* Oxford: A&C Black.

Henry De Lubac, 1960, *The Discovery of God,* Edinburgh: T&T Clark.

Glenn Ward, 2003, *Teach Yourself Postmodernism,* London: Hodder & Stoughton.

Pete Ward (ed.), 1999, *Mass Culture,* Oxford: Bible Reading Fellowship.

Peter Ward (ed.), 2004, *The Rite Stuff,* Oxford: Bible Reading Fellowship.

Mark Yaconelli, 2006, *Contemplative Youth Ministry: Practising the Presence of Jesus with Young People,* London: SPCK.

Notes

1 The incumbent of the parish of the Holy Spirit, Southsea, Canon Fr Michael Lewis SSC is a deeply inspirational priest with the wisdom and conviction to simply let his curate work unhindered. I remain forever in his debt.

2 As the priest makes the bread and wine into (literally, for many of us) the body and blood of Our Lord, he or she lifts it and shows it to the congregation. Traditionally, this is marked by the ringing of a bell to draw attention to it.

3 It is an essential principle of Blesséd that everything is given away. This is not least because of its cavalier attitude to intellectual property – a key value of the digitally literate, but because it is seen as a gift from God to be shared. The video sharing website YouTube is the key mechanism to deliver that efficiently to a wide-range of people. You can't charge for admission to the Mass and maybe that is why Blesséd is a poor, underfunded destitute little urchin of a group.

15

A Story of Anglimergence:
Community, Covenant, Eucharist
and Mission at Church of the
Apostles

KAREN WARD

Church of the Apostles (COTA), based in Seattle, USA, is an intentional, sacramental community in the way of Jesus Christ, and a ministry of the Episcopal Diocese of Olympia, WA. Over the past seven years of our existence, we have continually discovered how our Anglican ethos and heritage provides deep and rich resources for engaging in ministry and mission in the postmodern age.

The title of the book by Duncan Dormor et al., *Anglicanism: The Answer to Modernity*, sums up my own view that the Anglican ethos, steeped in community, covenant, Eucharist and mission, has the capacity to address the deepest longings of postmodern seekers for meaning, purpose, and spiritual food for the mind, body, heart and soul.

In January 2008 I founded a website and online Anglican community called Anglimergent (Ward, 2008). On its pages I have described Anglimergents as:

appreciative of the rich heritage of our Anglican way of being Christian, and how Anglicanism (when released from modern strictures) is deeply resonate (sic) with the hungers people have for authentic community, intellectual honesty, deep tradition, ancient-future spiritual practice, and servant-hood in the way of Jesus. As the original 'third way' (via media) within Christianity, and as a diverse, multi-cultural and global communion, Anglicanism is uniquely poised to engage the imaginations of emerging generations and all spiritual seekers in today's world.

We are excited to give fresh expression and renewed missional praxis to the Anglican way of being Christian, to mentor (sic) support, bless and release 'next generation' leaders, and bring the massive spiritual riches of our tradition to bear in (sic) emerging culture and engaging (sic) emerging generations in intentional, sacramental community around Jesus Christ.

I began, in the year 2000, to have dreams about a new kind of church that could welcome spiritually seeking postmoderns not already connected to church, without requiring them to check their culture at the door. I began to dream online by launching a modest website called www.emergingchurch.org (years before the term 'emerging church' became common parlance), to share my ideas. In 2002 the Diocese of Olympia, in partnership with the local Lutheran synod, invested in my dream and authorized the start up of this new ministry. It was to be a sort of 'mission lab', a small, local, fresh expression of church 'communitas', grounded in a theology of the Holy Trinity. It would mine the riches of Anglican liturgy and spiritual practice, along with materials from contemporary culture, to resource emerging Christian community and mission in the postmodern age.

I was convinced that Anglo-Catholic ritual, practice and sacramental mysticism – when brought into dialogue with contemporary art, culture and media, and in the context of a welcoming and 'culturally fluent' community – could provide space and place for postmodern seekers to fall in love with God, form community with one another and then practice extending God's love to the surrounding neighbourhood.

We began in 2002 as a house church of six twenty-somethings, accompanied by one thirty-something priest. We had no manual for how to start a church; all we had were dreams of God and a deep desire to love God, one another and our neighbours, and to participate with God in the healing and redemption of the world. We began by meeting each Wednesday evening to reflect on the Scriptures, and in particular the Book of Acts and the parables of Jesus.

The Book of Acts showed us what the earliest intentional, sacramental community in the way of Jesus Christ was like, and how those who were baptized into Christ were formed and sustained for mission, 'devoting themselves to the apostles' teaching and fellowship, to the breaking of bread and the prayers' (Acts 2.42).

The parables of Jesus – especially of the Prodigal Son and the Wedding Banquet, showed us that the Kingdom or Reign of God is like a feast, where all are invited in and welcomed. It is the Holy Communion in God's divine life (seen in the Trinity) extended to embrace humanity, inviting our participation in God, and in God's healing and redeeming of the world. We were struck by the lengths that God went to to extend this embrace, to save and redeem us upon the cross, to call and adopt us through the covenant of baptism, and to nourish and form us for servant mission through the Eucharist.

We soon realized that the pattern of our gatherings was already reflective of the ancient pattern of the earliest Christian liturgy: we *gathered* in the name of Christ; we reflected upon the *Word* of God in the Scriptures; we prayed grace over a shared *meal*; we made *intercession* for needs of the world; and we were *sent forth* back into our daily lives to live into the pattern of these good things. We also realized that our calling as a community was to participate in God, meaning that we are called to become fully human (Imago Dei) and as such to participate with God's mission (Missio Dei).

Then we realized we were already monastic, because to be Anglican, in practice, is to be Benedictine: maintaining the rhythm of the church year, the rhythm of the weekly Eucharist and the diurnal rhythm of the daily office. And in terms of baptisms, we are part of a covenant community, the Order of Jesus (everyone who is baptized into Christ, puts on Christ). Here our primary 'rule' is the Baptismal Covenant from the Book of Common Prayer of the Episcopal Church, 1929, which is not unlike the baptismal liturgies of many different Christian denominations.

In this 'rule', we promise, with God's help, to continue in the apostles' teaching and fellowship, in the breaking of bread, and in the prayers; to persevere in resisting evil, and, whenever we fall into sin, repent and return to the Lord; to proclaim by word and example the Good News of God in Christ; to seek and serve Christ in all persons, loving our neighbour as ourselves; to strive for justice and peace among all people; and to respect the dignity of every human being.

We then discerned our calling to serve the neighbourhood of Fremont, the historic arts district of Seattle, and the most unchurched area of the city. In many ways, Seattle, and other cities in the Northwest, such as Portland and Vancouver, BC, have more in common with the post-Christian cities of Europe than with the church-going Midwestern and southern regions of the United States. To engage our frontline mission work, we morphed from being a house church into a 'shop front mission', operating a non-profit coffee shop, tea bar and performance gallery called 'The Living:Room'.

The headquarters of Starbucks coffee are located in Seattle, and on any given Sunday morning there are many more people in coffee shops than in churches; we decided to juxtapose the two. The mission statement of 'The Living:Room' was to provide 'a space for life'. By offering tea, coffee, Internet access and scones by day, and poetry, film and music in the evening, we were extending God's love and hospitality to our neighbours in ways that people of any faith, or none, could receive it. Being an intentional Christian community, we also held a Eucharist each and every Saturday evening in the café – our current practice to this day – calling it 'a vigil Mass of the resurrection'.

In 2006, we made our next big pilgrimage – across the street. We moved out of the shop front, closed 'The Living:Room' and wheeled our modest belongings across the street and into an old, empty church. We knew from church history that abbeys functioned as the community centres, or village commons, of pre-modern European villages; so, an old church that others saw as dilapidated and awaiting destruction or conversion into upmarket flats, we saw as the raw material for a new monastic, urban, abbey church.

After a year of renovation, with financial help from our diocese and the Lutheran synod, 'Fremont Abbey' now houses a fully functioning anchorite community of 150 apostles engaged in mission. The Abbey is a 'third place' and a 'co-op': it is a third place (a term coined by Ray Oldenberg in his book, *The Great Good Place*) because it is a space outside of home and work where people gather to experience renewed human community; it is a co-op in that it houses a community arts centre, a community café and a church community (COTA).

There is a clear link for us between the common prayer, sacramental spirituality and servant mission, all based in our Abbey. Frank Weston, Bishop of Zanzibar, aware of the deep connection between liturgy, mission and justice, admonished those at the 1923 Anglo-Catholic Congress to:

> Come out from before your tabernacles [containing reserved Sacrament]. You cannot claim to worship Jesus in the table if you do not pity Jesus in the slum ... If you say that an Anglo-Catholic has a right to hold his peace while his fellow citizens are living in hovels beneath the level of the streets, then I say to you that you do not know the Lord Jesus in his Sacrament.
> (Leech, 1981, p. 21)

I view what we do at COTA as being grounded in the insights of early Anglo-Catholicism (and first-century Christianity before it), in that we link liturgy, mission and justice. We juxtapose this catholic sacramentality, which is also resourced by the insights of monasticism, with the post-Christian, spiritual-but-not-religious, postmodern culture of urban Seattle.

As a postmodern, emerging, Anglo-Catholic new monastic community, full, active, and conscious participation in the weekly eucharistic liturgy is our main source of communal spiritual formation and mission orientation. Also, our liturgy is truly the work of the people, having emerged fresh from our community, whilst remaining ancient in shape.

In his book, *The Life of the Beloved*, Henri Nouwen writes of how Christian life and mission have a eucharistic shape, with God taking us, blessing us, breaking us and giving us for the life of the world (1992, pp. 48–9). For me, our eucharistic mission is captured most succinctly in one of the Offertory Sentences of the 1979 Prayer Book, which says: 'Walk in love as Christ loved us and gave himself for us an offering and sacrifice to God' (Episcopal Church, 1979, p. 376).

A liturgy by COTA is available on the SCM-Canterbury Press website. Go to https:/www.scm-canterburypress.co.uk/bookdetails.asp?ISBN=9781853111973. In response to the missional priority of the Anglican Communion, of engaging God's mission and justice through participation with the United Nations Millennium Development Goals (MDGs), a young student from COTA named Matthew Lyon envisioned this fresh expression of Anglican liturgy. It is a great example of how fresh expressions of Anglican community, liturgy and sacramentality serve God's mission to heal and redeem the world. It is a small gift from COTA in Seattle, to the wider Anglican Communion, and to all who may find it helpful.

References

Duncan Dormor, Jack McDonald and Jeremy Caddick, 2006, *Anglicanism: The Answer to Modernity*, London: Continuum.

Episcopal Church, 1979, Book of Common Prayer, New York City: Seabury Press.

Kenneth Leech, 1981, *The Social God*, London: Sheldon Press.

Henri Nouwen, 1992, *The Life of the Beloved*, New York City: Crossroad Publishing.

Ray Oldenberg, 2008, *The Great Good Place*, New York City: Marlowe & Co, 1989.

Karen Ward, 2008, *About*, viewed on 2 January 2009 at http://anglimergent.ning.com/page/page/show?id=1972049%3APage%3A7761

16

Concluding Thoughts

ABBOT STUART BURNS OSB

Back in 1833 the Church of England was in a pretty sorry state, in all respects. It was very much regarded as a wing of the political establishment – to the point that the Parliament in Westminster proposed the suppression of several of the Irish bishoprics. This prompted John Keble to preach as he did in the Assize Sermon in Oxford that year. His sermon gave birth to what became known as the Oxford Movement, which was to have the most amazing effect on the life of the Church throughout the country and well beyond – something no one could have imagined, let alone foreseen. Others took up the seed sown by Keble, and the 'Catholic Revival' within Anglicanism was under way.

Keble's message was that the Church isn't an arm of the State; it is a divine creation: God's work, Christ's body on earth, here to continue Jesus' ministry. His message struck at the roots of much of the sickness of the institutional Church, not least its divisions: Christ has only one body and that can't be divided; neither can the worship of heaven be divided from worship on earth. Worship – not the formal reading of prayers and services, but the joyful expression of Christ's love for the Father in the power of the Spirit – can't be separated from a care for God's people, especially those close to Christ's heart: the poor and the marginalized. 'Whatever you do to the least ... you do to me' (Matt. 25.40). 'It isn't those who cry "Lord, Lord", who will enter the Kingdom of Heaven but those who do the will of my Father' (Matt. 7.21).

There followed a flowering of wonderful, worshipful liturgy and heroic, sacrificial ministry in the slums of the big cities, as the Church began again to share Christ's passion for the poor and for justice. Over the next one hundred years or so, came a powerful force in the transformation of the Church – the recovery of the sacramental life. This included a greater care for liturgy and for church buildings, concern for mission in its many forms, the re-establishment of the religious orders, the training of the clergy and a serious concern for the unity of Christ's Church.

Then, in the middle of the last century, a huge paradigm shift began in Western society, and with it seemed to come a dimming of the passion of the early days; the wonderful liturgies began to ring hollow and the joy and compassion were replaced, as Archbishop Rowan has said, by a fussy kind of churchiness, and a wordiness, which has often served to diminish people's perception of God.

As we know, elsewhere the Holy Spirit was at work, building on some of the insights of the catholic revival, calling people back to the Scriptures again and to a more spontaneous kind of worship. People began exploring more deeply the implications of what it meant to be the Body of Christ on earth; they discovered a vaster and more inclusive God; they recovered the expectation of the ministry of all the baptized, and the value of meeting in small groups for prayer and study; they rediscovered Christianity as a way of life rather than a religion.

In our liturgy we now affirm that 'We are the Body of Christ'. The penny is slowly dropping that this isn't just a pious phrase but it is 'for real'. It's about each of us living the Christ-life: allowing Christ to live and work in and through us, following the path of Jesus to whatever version of Calvary is for us. It will cost not less than everything, but Jesus promises the hundred-fold (Luke 8.8) and the joy of eternal life. Slowly we are waking up to the fact that eternal life is for now, not just after we die.

It seems that God has brought us to the threshold of something that promises to be more powerful and wonderful than anything the Church has known for centuries. Perhaps the most important thing we need to hear, and Archbishop Rowan has underlined this, is that it is God's work and not ours. We can choose to work with God, with all the risks that will entail, or we can hold back and opt to cling onto the familiar, with all the dire risks that will entail.

Several chapters in this book have highlighted the fact that there is a growing hunger in society for an authentic spirituality. Sadly, the last place most people think of looking for this is in a parish church; but for those who do, what do they find? Do they encounter a group of people on fire with the joy of the Christ-life? Are they met with the eyes of compassion, as people in need were, when they met Jesus?

The language and the imagery of the prayers, readings and hymns may well seem very alien to people in this age of the world-wide web, space travel and genetic research. There may be little to alert them to the fact that most of the language is that of poetry and metaphor, and isn't intended to be taken literally. They may be mystified by the rituals that many churchgoers take for granted. If they manage to connect at all, do those who turn to the Church in crisis find nourishment and hope?

It's so important to remember that what counted as an appropriate response to God in one generation and culture will be very different in another. We need to be free to explore fresh ways of hearing the gospel imperatives for the situations in which we find ourselves now; new ways of hearing the radical things Jesus was trying to say in his day, which people weren't ready to hear, and applying them now, to where we are. Remember, the disciples were with Jesus day in, day out, for three years, and still they persisted in getting hold of the wrong end of every stick Jesus gave them. It's no wonder the generations that have followed have been slow to grasp his meaning and have often mistakenly taken his metaphors literally.

Archbishop Rowan has written of the need for non-verbal as well as verbal expressions of faith – we need fresh symbols and metaphors as we try to grasp and communicate the mystery of our faith. These, I suspect, will only come as we are silent and empty in front of the mystery we call God.

Ann Lewin wrote a short verse when she was staying in our monastery some years ago:

Pause at the threshold,
Of the sacred space.
Bow low.
Prepare for fresh encounter,
With the Holy One.

It's that encounter with the Holy One which will transform us (although it will never be what we are expecting), and it will go on transforming us as we are drawn deeper and deeper into communion with God as God is: the God who fills all things, who created the vastness of the universe and the delicacy of a spider's web; the God who is nothing like any of our expectations or definitions and who is present at every moment, in every situation.

It's good to remember Moses' experience when he came to the Burning Bush. 'Tell me your name', he asked. 'I am who I am', was the reply (Ex. 3.14). Which could well be rendered, 'I am, and no human mind will ever be able to understand.' This God meets us in the silence, even though the experience usually feels more like absence than presence, because we simply don't have the mental furniture to process the experience. He patiently strips us of our misconceptions, and opens us to receive a larger vision. Archbishop Rowan Williams has a lovely passage towards the end of his book *Tokens of Trust*:

At the prosaic and daily level, it can involve a great deal of sitting there facing frustration and doubt of the most acute sort: God calls me to delight and eternal fulfilment – so why exactly am I sitting here twiddling my thumbs, shifting from buttock to buttock, and wondering where and what and who God is?
(Williams, 2007, p. 156)

It takes time – a lot of time – to get to the point where we can allow God to be who God is, rather than what we would like God to be. This God, who meets us in our neighbour, challenges us to recognize the sacredness of other people, and especially those we find difficult, and to receive them as gift. This God meets us as we worship and as we ponder the familiar Scriptures again and again, alone and with others, inviting us to hear what we have never heard before. This God excites our imagination, giving us fresh awareness that the whole of life and creation is being caught up in the God who is. God invites us to reassess our whole understanding of the Good News Jesus came to bring.

If, as the Epistle to the Ephesians says, 'Christ fills all things' (1.23), if God really is 'all in all', if our God is inclusive, rather than an exclusive, cultic god, then it may be that we need to re-examine our attitude to people of other faiths, and of none. We may need to examine our attitude to our possessions and lifestyle: if our Christ was, and is, starving and homeless, might he be inviting us to travel through this world a bit lighter and know the joy of sharing what we have?

And it's that joy that is the real hallmark of someone who is allowing Christ to live in them. As Archbishop Rowan said in his address to the Millennium Conference of Anglican Religious, at Swanwick in the year 2000, 'Joy is where God happens.' Wherever there is joy there will be fresh expressions of God's love made flesh. Our God is, after all, Emmanuel, God with us in all the wonderful and ever-changing mess of life.

Reference

Rowan Williams, 2007, *Tokens of Trust: An Introduction to Christian Belief*, London: Canterbury Press.

The Contributors

Ian Adams is a priest in the Church of England, and leader of maybe, an emerging church community in Oxford. As an Associate Missioner with Fresh Expressions, and in partnership with CMS, he also supports and mentors other new missional communities. He is a Living Faith trainer for the Diocese of Oxford, a part-time chaplain and tutor at the Oxford Centre for Youth Ministry, and leader of a project called 'Pace Bene', which is aimed at helping individuals and communities live more simply, creatively and peacefully, and to engage with the possibility of God. He helps people explore this imaginatively, particularly through contemplative prayer, stilling practices and symbolic actions.

Christopher Ashley is a leader at The Crossing, the emergent Christian community based at the Cathedral Church of St Paul in Boston, Massachusetts. He is completing a Master of Divinity at Harvard Divinity School in Cambridge, Massachusetts, and plans to pursue doctoral work on the role of blessing in Christian community.

Paige Blair served as rector of St George's Episcopal Church in York, Maine, USA, until May 2009 and is now rector of St Peter's Episcopal Church in Del Mar, California. As a leader in Episcopalians for Global Reconciliation, she is passionately committed to the movement to Make Poverty History. Because of her work as an iconographer in the Byzantine tradition, and her passion for challenging the Church to minister effectively

to all generations, she is regularly invited to teach in parishes and dioceses throughout The Episcopal Church.
www.e4gr.org
www.millenniumcampaign.org
www.whiteband.org
www.one.org

Thomas Brackett is the Program Officer for Church Planting and Ministry Redevelopment at the Episcopal Church Center in New York City. Originally ordained as a Baptist, Tom worked with cell group ministries in the 1980s and explored liturgical renewal and culturally-sensitive evangelism on other continents. Since his ordination in The Episcopal Church, he has planted churches, revitalized a campus ministry, served as an interim rector, led a turn-around process in a rural Maine ambulance service and recently served as the vicar of a diocesan homeless ministry in Asheville, North Carolina.

Stuart Burns was ordained in 1969 and, after a varied ministry in urban and rural parishes and university chaplaincy, he became a Benedictine monk in 1989 and was elected abbot in 1996. His community of nuns and monks is currently 'in transit' from Burford, Oxfordshire, to a new ecologically sustainable monastery near Worcester. While the new monastery is being built, the Community is asking, 'How does God want us to express the monastic life for the 21st Century?'

Stephen Cottrell is the Bishop of Reading. He has worked in parishes in London and Chichester, as Pastor of Peterborough Cathedral, as Missioner in the Wakefield diocese and as part of Springboard, the Archbishop's evangelism team. He has written widely about evangelism, spirituality and discipleship. Among his recent books are *From the Abundance of the Heart: Catholic Evangelism for all Christians* (DLT, 2006); *Do Nothing to Change your Life: Discovering What Happens When You Stop* (CHP, 2007); *Hit the Ground Kneeling: Seeing Leadership Differently* (CHP, 2008), and a book of Lent and Holy Week meditations, *The Things He Carried* (SPCK, 2008). He is married to Rebecca and they have three boys.

Richard Giles worked as a parish priest in England for over 30 years before serving as Dean of Philadelphia Cathedral in the Diocese of Pennsylvania 1999–2008. His particular expertise in the design of liturgical space bore fruit in the publication of *Re-Pitching the Tent* (2004), now in its third edition, *Creating Uncommon Worship* (2004) and *Times and Seasons* (2008). Other titles include *Mark my Word, How to be an Anglican,* and *Here I Am*, all from Canterbury Press. In 2008 he became a Visiting Fellow of St John's College, Durham. He now lives in Tynemouth, and works part-time as a consultant in the renewal of liturgy and parish life.
www.liturgyworks.org.uk

Marie Harkey is a leader at The Crossing, the emergent Christian community based at the Cathedral Church of St Paul in Boston, Massachusetts. She is a student at Episcopal Divinity School in Cambridge, Massachusetts, and is passionate about teaching how liturgy shapes community.

Tessa Holland is a priest, Quiet Garden host, retreat leader and spiritual director in the diocese of Chichester. She lives as a contemplative-in-action in the context of family life, and is a member of the core team of Contemplative Fire and regional chaplain for The Quiet Garden Movement.

Brian McLaren is an author, speaker, blogger, networker and activist. He began his career as a college English instructor, and then worked as a church-planter and pastor for 24 years. He currently serves on the board of directors for Sojourners and Emergent Village and is an avid supporter of several other non-profits. His books include *A New Kind of Christian* (Josey Bass, 2008), *A Generous Orthodoxy* (Zondervan, 2006), *The Secret Message of Jesus* (Nelson Bibles, 2007), *Everything Must Change* (Nelson Books, 2008), and *Finding Our Way Again*

(W Publishing, 2008). He travels widely, and makes his home near Washington, DC. He and his wife Grace have four adult children.
www.brianmclaren.net
www.emergentvillage.com
www.sojo.net

Ian Mobsby is an ordained Church of England Priest Missioner, currently with the Moot Community in London, UK, with over 20 years' experience of working with various emerging and fresh expressions of church. He lectures on emerging and fresh expressions of church in the USA, Canada, New Zealand, Australia and Europe, and is currently a core team member of the Archbishop's Fresh Expressions team. As such, he chairs a national round table that seeks to promote and develop fresh expressions of the catholic and contemplative traditions. His two books are entitled *Emerging and Fresh Expressions of Church* (Moot Community Publishing, 2008) and *The Becoming of G-d* (Lulu Press, 2008).

Philip Roderick is a priest, percussionist, educator and speaker. He is founder-director of The Quiet Garden Movement (www. quietgarden.co.uk) and leader of Contemplative Fire. Philip is the author of *Beloved: Conversations with Henri Nouwen* (Canterbury Press, 2007); the producer of 'Sacred Posture', a DVD teaching body prayer; and 'Sheer Sound', a CD featuring the ambient Hang Drum.

After finishing his training **Simon Rundell** worked in urban Portsmouth at the Church of the Holy Spirit, Southsea. Since 2004 he has been the Priest-in-Charge of the parish of St Thomas the Apostle in Elson, Gosport. Passionately committed to mission, youth work and the sacramental life, Simon takes the blame for 'Blesséd', an alt.worship experiment which has been skulking around the back of the Church of England since 2002. It is a highly multi-sensory, immersive worship experience which is deeply eucharistic, outrageously Anglo-Catholic and wildly, rabidly inclusive. To witness the achievements of the past and to become a part of the future, see www.blessed.org.uk.

Stephanie Spellers is Priest and Lead Organizer at The Crossing, an emergent Christian community based at the Cathedral Church of St Paul in Boston, Massachusetts. She is also the author of *Radical Welcome: Embracing God, The Other and the Spirit of Transformation* (Church Publishing, 2006). A consultant and co-chair of The Episcopal Church's Standing Commission on Mission and Evangelism, Stephanie travels the country encouraging faith communities that seek to embrace transformation, reckon with their fear of change and welcome cultural groups that mainline churches often hold at the margins. www.thecrossingboston.org

Phyllis Tickle is a Senior Fellow of Cathedral College at the Washington National Cathedral and a founding member of The Canterbury Roundtable. She is an authority on religion in North America and a popular lecturer on the subject. She is the author of some two dozen books on religion, and most recently of *The Great Emergence: How Christianity is Changing and Why* (Baker Book House, 2008).

Carl Turner is Precentor of Exeter Cathedral and responsible for its worship and music. A member of the General Synod he is also a member of the Liturgical Commission. Ordained in 1985, Carl was a parish priest until 2001, serving for 11 years in a major East London parish alongside the Society of St Francis. A regular contributor to Roots Magazine, he also leads conferences and retreats and facilitates groups in the area of mission, worship and spirituality. He has worked with Springboard and ReSource.
www.exeter-cathedral.org.uk
www.transformingworship.co.uk

Michael Volland has a BA in Fine Art. He spent six years working as a youth minister during which time he studied for an MA in Theological Education at King's College London. In 2004 he moved to Cambridge with his family to study at Ridley Hall Theological College. While at Ridley his first book, *God on the Beach*, was published by Survivor (2005). Michael was ordained deacon and pioneer minister in 2006. He is currently the assistant curate at Gloucester cathedral, and priest to the feig community which he pioneered (www.feig.org.uk). He is reading for a Doctorate at King's College London.

Sue Wallace has worked for Visions since 1992 as music and arts co-ordinator. She was brought up Roman Catholic and became Anglican at the age of 17. She is the author of four books published by Scripture Union, including *Multi-Sensory Prayer* (2000), which has now sold 10,000 copies. Sue studied music and education at Christ Church Canterbury and, under the name of 'Abbess', writes and composes music that blends technology and ancient prayers. In recent years she trained for ordination on the Northern Ordination Course, and was priested in July 2007.

Karen M. Ward is the founder and vicar of Church of the Apostles, Seattle, a seven-year-old emerging church community in the Episcopal Diocese of Olympia, Washington. She is also the founder of Anglimergent.org, 'a generous and generative friendship among diverse Anglicans, engaging with the emerging church and mission'.
www.apostlechurch.org
www.anglimergent.org

Kirsten Wesselhoeft is a leader at The Crossing, the emergent Christian community based at the Cathedral Church of St Paul in Boston, Massachusetts. Raised a Mennonite, Kirsten has also been active at Imago Dei, an emergent community in Portland, Oregon. She is graduate of Harvard Divinity School in Cambridge, Massachusetts, and is currently pursuing a doctorate in comparative ethics at Harvard University, with an emphasis on Christianity and Islam.

Rowan Williams is the Archbishop of Canterbury. In 2004 he established Fresh Expressions, an Archbishops' initiative across the Church of England, to encourage fresh expressions of church as a normal part of every diocese and tradition, within a mixed economy of church life.